SPIRITUAL BLESSING

Spiritual Blessing

The Path to True Happiness

D. Martyn Lloyd-Jones

KINGSWAY PUBLICATIONS
EASTBOURNE

ISBN 0 85476 806 8

Co-published in South Africa with
SCB Publishers
Cornelis Struik House, 80 McKenzie Street
Cape Town 8001, South Africa
Reg no 04/02203/06

Designed and produced by Bookprint Creative Services
P.O. Box 827, BN21 3YJ, England for
KINGSWAY PUBLICATIONS
Lottbridge Drove, Eastbourne, E. Sussex BN23 6NT.
Printed in Great Britain.

Contents

1. The Person of Jesus Christ   9

2. Trust and Obey   31

3. The Nature of the Blessing   53

4. A Transforming Blessing   76

5. A Superabundance of Blessing   96

6. The Cleansing of the Temple   116

7. The Temple of the Living God   135

8. Seeking Signs   155

9. True or Temporary Believers?   175

10. A Personal Relationship   195

11. A Temple of His Body   215

12. The Captain's Inspection   234

*These sermons were first
preached by Dr Martyn Lloyd-Jones
at Westminster Chapel between
October and December 1965*

1

The Person of Jesus Christ

And when they wanted wine, the mother of Jesus saith unto him, They have no wine. Jesus saith unto her, Woman, what have I to do with thee? mine hour is not yet come. His mother saith unto the servants, Whatsoever he saith unto you, do it.   John 2:3–5

As I call your attention to this second chapter of John, I want to make my purpose clear. I am not concerned to expound every single verse. Instead, my aim is to bring out the great theme of John's Gospel which it is John's whole purpose to convey to us. At the end of his Gospel John says, 'And many other signs truly did Jesus in the presence of his disciples, which are not written in this book: but these are written, that ye might believe that Jesus is the Christ, the Son of God; and that believing ye might have life through his name' (John 20:30). That is John's theme, this 'life' that it is possible for us to receive 'through his name'.

John's theme is perhaps never stated more gloriously than in the words of our Lord himself: 'I am come that they might have life, and that they might have it more abundantly' (John 10:10). That is what we are interested in, that is what we are concerned about, this life more abundant, this abounding life, which has been made available to us by the coming of the Son of God into this world.

Obviously the first thing we must do is understand who this Jesus of Nazareth is. That is the fundamental question. Who is he? What is he? And that is why John begins his Gospel with that great prologue in the first eighteen verses: 'In the beginning was the Word, and the Word was with God, and the Word was God' (verse 1). But then we read, 'And the Word was made flesh, and dwelt among us' (verse 14). This is the profound doctrine of the Christian faith. If we are not clear about who Jesus is, then we shall never know anything about the life which he came to give, and certainly we shall never know it in the abundance that we are meant to experience. So we are given a tremendous portrayal of him, and his glory, and his purpose in coming into this world. 'He came unto his own, and his own received him not. But as many as received him, to them gave he power to become the sons of God' (verses 11–12). That is it! That is what we are meant to be: 'sons of God', enjoying his life in all its fullness and abundance.

Then let us look at the second section of this great first chapter of John's Gospel – verses 19 to the end. Here a tremendous emphasis is put upon the fact that our Lord has come to baptise us with his Holy Spirit. John the Baptist contrasts himself with our Lord. John, the first great witness to him, the forerunner, says, 'I am not the Christ . . . there standeth one among you, whom ye know not . . . the same is he which baptizeth with the Holy Ghost' (verses 20, 26, 33). And if we are not clear about that, we shall know nothing about this 'life more abundant' which we are meant to be enjoying as Christian people. It is not God's purpose for us to shuffle through this world, but to abound with life, and with glory, and to share in his great abundance. That is the contrast John gives us.

A second, and similar, contrast is seen in verse 17: 'The law was given by Moses, but grace and truth came by Jesus Christ.' This is a tremendous contrast between the old and the new, and in John's Gospel the characteristic of the new is always abundance.[1] This is the whole emphasis of this Gospel, as it is, of course, of all the New Testament.

At the end of the first chapter we are given small cameos in which we are shown how our Lord begins to call to himself and instruct certain men who will be able to carry on the giving of his message after he has returned to heaven – it is the formation of the church which is established on the foundation of the apostles and prophets. There is great comfort in the realisation that our Lord calls all types of men and women, that he calls us in different ways, and that, indeed, it does not matter very much who we are nor what we are. What matters is who he is, and what he is, and what he can

---

[1] These verses are dealt with by Dr Lloyd-Jones in *Joy Unspeakable*, Kingsway, 1983.

make of us. So we see him calling these different men and beginning to prepare them for their work of continuing the preaching of this great message which he came into the world to bring. And the church, when she has really functioned as the church, has been doing that ever since, and her message is the same: it is always about this life more abundant.

So we must keep all this in our minds as we look at John's second chapter. It is important to remember that our Lord continues to teach and act today just as he taught and acted when he was here in the days of his flesh. So often we read the Bible to no profit because we read it as if it were some ancient history. We say: 'This happened then, that's all right, but, of course, today our circumstances are different.' That is quite wrong. The whole point of the New Testament is to tell us that what he did on earth, he merely *began* to do. Luke, therefore, introduces the Acts of the Apostles with the words: 'The former treatise have I made, O Theophilus, of all that Jesus began both to do and teach' (Acts 1:1). That means he has not finished. He began while he was here on earth and, having returned to heaven, where he is seated at the right hand of God's glory, he continues to act.

In our Bibles, Luke's book is called the 'Acts of the Apostles'. Some people say we should call it the 'Acts of the Holy Spirit' but I maintain that Luke says we should call it 'the Acts of the Risen Lord'. When Peter and John healed the man at the Beautiful Gate of the Temple, and the crowd came admiring and ready to worship them, Peter said, 'Why look ye so earnestly on us, as though by our own power or holiness we had made this man to walk?' (Acts 3:12). And then he said, 'The God of Abraham, and of Isaac, and of Jacob, the God of our fathers, hath glorified his Son Jesus ... And his name through faith in his name hath made this man strong ... yea, the faith which is by him hath given him this perfect soundness in the presence of you all' (Acts 3:13, 16). It is the Jesus whom you have crucified and rejected, he is the One who has done this.

The value of the Gospels, therefore, is that they tell us in a most interesting, human, historical, factual manner what our Lord is like, how he deals with people and how he gives them these great blessings. We are shown who he is in a simple, pictorial manner that we can easily grasp.

As we read the accounts of the various incidents of our Lord's life, we must remember that they are parables also, and that their object is to tell us that what he did then he is still doing and can do for us. He is still the same, only more so because he is now glorified. The Gospels tell us the kind of thing that our Lord is ready to do for us, and the way in which he is ready to do it. They are not only history; they are more than history. They are a living message coming to us in our problems and perplexities.

So let us look at the wedding in Cana of Galilee where there is a problem, a difficulty, in connection with the wedding feast. Let us see how our Lord solves it, and let us remember that as our Lord came to the marriage in Cana of Galilee and transformed the whole situation, he is here today to do for us something infinitely bigger and greater. He is here and, just as at Cana in Galilee, he is here to bless.

Now the marriage feast at Cana of Galilee is interesting for many reasons. We are told by John, 'This beginning of miracles did Jesus in Cana of Galilee, and manifested forth his glory; and his disciples believed on him' (verse 11): that is his purpose. This miracle is the first, and therefore it is of great interest. In the original Greek the word that John uses for 'miracle' is 'sign'. John writes: 'This beginning of signs . . .' Our Lord changes the water into wine as a *sign* of his glory.

Now I am not primarily concerned to give you an analysis of the miracle. I must do that, of course, but I do it simply in order to get at the message. It is the message we need. I shall not entertain you with a discussion about miracles, and about whether we can reconcile miracles with scientific knowledge. That is how people often handle these matters and they miss the glory. While they argue cleverly about miracles they miss the Christ, and they miss the blessing. Knowing nothing about abundant life, in spite of all their cleverness, they go back to a life of sin and failure.

But let me say this in passing: at the wedding in Cana we see a perfect illustration of what is meant by a miracle. A miracle is a supernatural action. It is an action which is above nature. It does not break the laws of nature but acts in a realm above.

This, of course, is interesting and important. The biblical view of the universe is that God made it and controls it. People talk cleverly about 'the laws of nature', but what does that phrase mean? Well, it simply means that God, the infinite, wise Creator, has made everything after a plan and after a pattern.

God works in an orderly manner. The late Sir James

Jeans said that his scientific studies had driven him to the conclusion that there must be a great Mind at the back of the universe. He said, 'God must be a great mathematician.' By that he meant that the more we investigate nature, the more we discover that it has a design, a pattern, a balance, an order, an arrangement. That is the astounding thing about our world. Are spring, summer, autumn, winter the result of chance? Obviously not. In the very constitution of things there is a governing principle and a process of cause and effect. Now all this has been put there by God, and is the result of his handiwork.

Usually the universe proceeds according to its laws. Take the way in which wine is normally made. Think of the life story of the grape, and the importance of the rain and the sunshine and so on. At the end the grapes are harvested, and the wine is produced. It works, as we said, according to 'the laws of nature', which is quite a good term as long as we remember that these laws have been put into nature by God.

The laws of nature operate throughout the whole of life. We see them at work in our growth and development, and in the healing process. If we cut into the skin, the incision will heal by a wonderful and complex process. The healing goes on slowly and regularly, unobtrusively, almost unobserved. We cannot see it happening, but suddenly we find that healing has taken place. That is how things normally happen.

What is a miracle? Well, it is when everything happens more quickly; it is the whole process speeded up. God, who has normally been acting through the laws which he has put into nature, suddenly acts independently of them and works directly instead of indirectly. In a miracle of healing, for example, the end result is the same healing. The difference lies in the way it has taken place.

Now I must emphasise that that is not all there is to a miracle, but in essence that is what a miracle is. Thus, in the wedding at Cana, the normal process whereby wine is produced is altogether speeded up. But there is more to this miracle than that; there is also the element of creation because our Lord starts with water only, and turns that water into wine. In other words, this act of God which we call a miracle is supernatural and it is creative.

I am always amazed that anybody who claims to believe in God should ever be troubled by the fact of miracles. If we believe in God at all, a miracle should not surprise us. Is God tied down by his own laws? Is God not free to act in any way he likes? Is God hemmed in by his own creation? The idea is quite ridiculous. If we believe in an almighty, eternal God, who is over all, then we must believe that there is no limit to what he may do. He normally chooses to act in an ordinary, orderly manner, but when it pleases him, he may give some manifestation of his glory and power in an unusual and exceptional manner. That is what we mean by a miracle, and that is what we see so prominently in the life of his Son. It is through these miracles that our Lord gives the signs which show that he is indeed the Son of God, this exceptional, this unique person. Miracles are attestations of his person and of his Godhead.

So here at the wedding in Cana we see the first sign

that our Lord ever gave. It applies to us in many ways. Our harvest thanksgiving, for instance, is an acknowledgement that crops do not grow and ripen automatically, but by God's laws.[1] In this service we are reminded of his bounty, his goodness and his kindness. Why should he feed us? Why should he give us health and strength? Do we deserve this? Is it because he is grateful for our obedience, and zeal for the glory of his name? No, no! The harvest is a manifestation of this bountiful Giver.

But what happens on the level of the material and physical is nothing but a pale shadow and suggestion of this infinitely bigger and more eternal work that God has done in the person of his Son. And that is the message that, as Christian people, we should always be seeking to give. 'The heavens declare the glory of God' (Psalm 19:1); the harvest declares the glory of God. Yes, and we thank God. But the harvest is a picture of what God does for us in the realm of the spirit. Each of us is body, mind and spirit. We thank God for every physical blessing, for health and strength and the possession of our faculties. We thank him for food and drink and clothing. We thank him for the blessings of the soul and mind – for the joy of knowledge, for the order of nature, and beauty of creation and so on. But oh, the blessings of the spirit! Men and women were created for these blessings. They alone are spirit. They alone are created in the image and likeness of God and they are meant to enjoy God. They are meant to share

---

[1] This was preached on Harvest Thanksgiving Sunday, 1965.

the life of God. They are meant to be partakers of the divine nature. Christ came in order to bring that about for us. We do not stop merely at the miracle of water turned into wine. We see a parable; we see something bigger. This is a sign. Our Lord is doing this to make us see who he is and what he can do for us. That must be the way in which we look at and consider this miracle.

To approach our Lord's miracles from a spiritual point of view does not mean that we forget the material and the physical blessings. As we said, we thank God for them. We are in the body, and there is a subtle inter-relationship between the mind and the body, spirit and matter. We must not separate them in a false way. We thank God for all his gifts, every one of them in every realm and department. It is no part of the Christian message to preach neglect of the body and to say that what happens in this material life does not matter. It does matter. The whole person is meant to be an expression of the glory of God. So we thank him for the flowers and for the sunshine. We thank him for all that he has given us so freely through another year, and we acknowledge our dependence upon his goodness, his kindness and his compassion. But we go on – we are in this other realm, and the question for us is: Do we know something about this life, and life more abundant that our Lord came to give? There is teaching about that in this miracle, and that is what we are going to see.

Let us begin by looking at what we are told here about our Lord himself. We must never forget that we are dealing with him. Christianity is not just a collection of teachings. It is that, but it is more than that. It is primarily and essentially a relationship to a person.

That is what we always tend to forget. At the present time there is almost a mania to know the Christian attitude towards this and the Christian attitude towards that, and our Lord himself has been entirely forgotten! But the one thing that matters is our relationship to him.

Someone has worked out a great Christian philosophy – all right! There is a Christian attitude to art – good! But do not get lost in that sort of thing, that is secondary. The vital issue is our Lord himself, and our relationship to him. And that is what dominates the whole situation here at Cana. We read, 'The third day there was a marriage in Cana of Galilee; and the mother of Jesus was there' (verse 1). Then comes the important point: 'And both Jesus was called, and his disciples, to the marriage' (verse 2). He is there.

As we read the New Testament, we find that uppermost in the minds of all the apostles was not so much what our Lord did for them, not what he enabled them to do, but he himself. The apostle Paul in particular always emphasises this: 'That I may know him, and the power of his resurrection' (Philippians 3:10). That is what Paul is after. It is not that he may work more miracles. No, no! 'That I may know him.' Paul says, 'I can do all things through Christ which strengtheneth me' (Philippians 4:13). 'For me to live is Christ' (Philippians 1:21). It is always our Lord. And since the whole object of the New Testament is to hold this person before us, and to present him to us, and to ask: 'What is your relationship to him?', it is astounding, is it not, that we can ever forget that?

So look at him as you find him here in John 2. Look

at the majesty of his person. Yes, he has come 'in the likeness of sinful flesh' (Romans 8:3). He has been working as a carpenter. He has not had the usual training given to teachers and leaders. Yet whenever he appears he dominates the scene. He stands out. Mark tells us: 'He could not be hid' (Mark 7:24). He comes incognito, in a very humble manner: 'The bruised reed shall he not break, and the smoking flax shall he not quench' (Isaiah 42:3). Yet in spite of that, the glory keeps on breaking through, and here it is dominating this entire scene.

Then the next thing we notice is that there is a mystery about him – all this is essential to our knowledge of him, that we may be blessed by him. He was born of the virgin Mary. He is the son of Mary, truly a man, and yet he does not address Mary as 'Mother', but as 'Woman', 'Lady', if you like. It is the same at the end of the Gospel when he is hanging on the cross. Furthermore, notice the question which he asks her: 'What have I to do with thee?' Then he says, 'Mine hour is not yet come.' What does all this mean?

There is only one adequate explanation: he is filled with a messianic consciousness. He knows who he is. He knows why he has come into this world. He realises that he is one apart. We find that stated more explicitly in other passages, but it is all here in embryo. This is the miracle and the marvel of this blessed person. He is a man among men, and yet he is not; there is always this apartness. He says, 'My God, and your God' (John 20:17); 'Ye are from beneath; I am from above' (John 8:23). He is in the world, he is one of us, he is truly man, and yet he is more. He is unique. He is separate. He shares in ordinary human relationships, he does have a mother, and yet it is not the ordinary relationship.

And then we notice another important thing about him: his intimate knowledge of us. He knows our very thoughts, desires and imaginations. He reads our mind. At the end of this chapter we are told that explicitly: 'Now when he was in Jerusalem at the passover, in the feast day, many believed in his name, when they saw the miracles which he did. But Jesus did not commit himself unto them, because he knew all men, and needed not that any should testify of man: for he knew what was in man' (John 2:23–25). Here his mother comes to him and says, 'They have no wine.' And immediately he knows exactly what is passing through her mind. Nothing is hidden from him.

Now there is a sense, of course, in which that is terrifying, but there is another sense in which it is most comforting, most soothing and consoling. Here is the blessed Son of God, and he knows us intimately and individually. He knows all about us – our fears, our cares, our problems, our anxieties, our difficulties, everything that passes within us. As the writer to the Hebrews says, 'For the word of God is quick, and powerful, and sharper than any twoedged sword, piercing even to the dividing asunder of the joints and marrow, and is a discerner of the thoughts and intents of the heart. Neither is there any creature that is not manifest in his sight. All things are naked and opened unto the eyes of him with whom we have to do' (Hebrews 4:12–13). And as the psalmist puts it about God the Father: 'Thou understandest my thought afar off' (Psalm 139:2).

Now I am emphasising this simply to ask a question: In your Christian life is that in your consciousness? Do you realise that? What is your Christianity? Is it just a number of propositions that you hold, or a number of things that you do, or is there this relationship, this intimate relationship, with a person, this consciousness that you are ever under his eye, and that all things that you do and think and even imagine are all known to him? This is absolutely vital if we are to know the real blessings of the Christian life.

And then I take you a step further and point out his great concern for us. Our Lord corrected his mother, and he corrects us. He is always watching, and he rebukes, he disciplines. All too often we stand in need of that. But he does it for our good, and the way he does it here is particularly instructive. He does correct Mary and rebuke her, and yet at the same time he offers encouragement, and she is quick to see that. We read that he says, 'Woman, what have I to do with thee? mine hour is not yet come.' And in response his mother says to the servants, 'Whatsoever he saith unto you, do it.' She has accepted the rebuke but she sees that there is something more.

And this is still true of our Lord. His object is eventually 'to present you faultless before the presence of his glory with exceeding joy' (Jude 24). He left the courts of heaven and came into this world, and taught, and lived, and died, and was buried, and rose again – what for? To bring us to God, to 'present us faultless'. So remember, 'Whom the Lord loveth he chasteneth, and scourgeth every son whom he receiveth' (Hebrews 12:6). We are in his hands, and must be ready for

rebukes and reprimands. He will pull us up. He will
stop us. He will indicate his displeasure. Do we live in
that sort of way? Are we aware of this? These, you see,
are the things that are taught us by this incident.

And lastly, of course, we are face to face with the tremendous fact of our Lord's power. That is why we are
here, and that is why I am preaching. 'I am not
ashamed of the gospel of Christ.' Why? 'It is the power
of God unto salvation to every one that believeth'
(Romans 1:16). 'Christ the power of God, and the
wisdom of God' (1 Corinthians 1:24). His power
shines out here.

Miracle?

Impossible!

Of course! That is why we are considering this
together. We need the miracle, every one of us, we need
the impossible, and it can happen. Here he is, filled
with pity joined with power. We must start with that.

But let us go on. Here he is, and there is hope for us
all in the glory of his divine Saviourhood. He is a perfect Saviour, a complete Saviour, and all that we need is
available to us in him. But wait a minute – we do not
enjoy this 'life more abundant'. Why not? It is because
we fall into errors. We make mistakes. And we see
some of our blunders as we look at the mother of Jesus
Christ.

Now many books have been written on Mary, and
especially on these remarks that our Lord makes to her.
It is an interesting and important subject. One section of
the so-called Christian church accords a unique position
to Mary and there are Christian people – Protestants,
evangelical people – who say, 'What does it matter?

We're all Christians. Let's all work together.'

Should we? Well, we can be taught from this incident. I want to show that Mary can sometimes be a hindrance to knowing the blessing that the Son of God has to give us. We must be careful. These things are absolutely vital. Our Lord rebuked Mary, and he rebukes all who follow her in her errors.

There are many people today who are seeking for a blessing and here is a great church that says to them, 'Come to us; trust us. Hand yourself over to the priesthood. We will pray to Mary for you.' And people go in their innocence and their ignorance and anxiety, thinking they will receive the blessing. But will they?

You see, this subject is very contemporary, it is very up-to-date. Yes, the wedding at Cana is history, but it is more, it still speaks to us in a living manner. So let us look at Mary. The first thing we find is that she has knowledge of his power. All credit to her. She knows what he can do. That is why she tells the servants, 'Whatsoever he saith unto you, do it.' How does she know? Well, you remember the story of the Annunciation. The angel Gabriel came to her and made astonishing statements about 'that holy thing' that was to be born of her (Luke 1:35). She never forgot that. We are told, 'Mary kept all these things, and pondered them in her heart' (Luke 2:19).

Then Mary remembered what happened when she visited her cousin Elizabeth, who was soon to give birth to John the Baptist. How could Mary forget it?

She remembered the words of ancient Simeon: 'Lord, now lettest thou thy servant depart in peace, according to thy word: for mine eyes have seen thy salvation'

(Luke 2:29–30). And she remembered the words of old Anna the prophetess. She hid them in her heart.

Mary knows that Jesus is unusual and exceptional, though at times she forgot. When Jesus was twelve years old Mary, Joseph and Jesus went up to Jerusalem. On the way home again, they suddenly realised that Jesus was not with their group. Mary was annoyed and hurried back, eventually finding Jesus arguing with and confuting the teachers in the Temple. She reprimanded him, and he replied to her, 'Wist ye not that I must be about my Father's business' (Luke 2:49). Mary never forgot that. And she watched him throughout the years: dutiful, growing. Yes, but there was always something different.

Then at the age of thirty Jesus left home and went to be baptised by John at the River Jordan. The Spirit descended, and John bore his witness to our Lord. That amazing man pointed to him and said: 'Behold the Lamb of God . . .' (John 1:29). Mary knows all this. She has observed all these things, and realises, therefore, that there is something strange and unusual, there is a power about him, a suggestion of the Almighty.

Mary is sure of his ability, as we see in the statement she makes to him: 'They have no wine.' And what she means, and he understands it at once, is this: 'The wine is running out. Do something about it.' Mary knows he can. She has confidence in his power. She merely makes the statement, 'They have no wine,' but what matters is the way she says it. 'Do something about it: you can, you must.'

Now much of this is excellent. In this way Mary bears her witness to our Lord's uniqueness and to the majesty of his power. But we notice her presumption, and this is what is emphasised here. Mary takes it upon herself to give him an order. She is trying to command him, trying to tell him what to do and when to do it. And this is of vital importance for us.

Mary's presumption stands out and our Lord at once rebukes her. Look at the rebuke: 'Woman.' Now do not misunderstand that. There is a danger of our taking that expression, 'Woman', as if it were derogatory. It is not. There is great politeness in it. As I have said, some suggest that we should translate it by the word 'Lady'. Our Lord is not dismissing Mary. But he is saying, 'Woman' – and why? Well, he is emphasising the uniqueness that belongs to him. She is his mother, and yet there are limits to that conception: Mary must realise that hers is a special, a unique kind of motherhood.

That comes out further in the next phrase: 'What have I to do with thee?' This is a difficult phrase from the linguistic, grammatical standpoint, but the meaning is quite plain. It literally reads, 'What is there to me and thee?' I rather like the suggestion here of the Amplified New Testament which puts it like this: 'What have we in common? Leave it to me.' You see the idea? Mary says in effect, 'They have no wine. I say you should do something about it.'

Our Lord responds, 'What have we in common? Leave it to me.'

Others have suggested that our Lord's reply should be put like this: 'Leave me to myself. Let me follow my own course.' Or again it could be rendered: 'This is my concern, not yours. We are not in partnership.'

Our Lord's meaning is brought out still more forcibly

by the words 'mine hour'. 'Mine hour is not yet come.'
Your hour has obviously come – you think I should do
this at once, and at your bidding, but my time has not
yet come.

Now we must not get confused about this. There are
further references to this 'hour' later on. Our Lord is
not referring to his death here, but means: The time for
me to do as you are suggesting has not yet come. Mary
must realise who he is. She must realise why he has
come into this world. Yes, he has, as it were, borrowed
her womb in order to be born as a man, but he is *God*.
He has been subject to her as a child and as a natural
person, yes, but he is more than that, and the time has
now come for him to enter on his great ministry. The
early time has ended; this time is beginning. He serves
God, and God has sent him on a mission and has given
him an 'hour', and told him what to do and when to do
it. Mary must no longer interfere, therefore. She has no
right to dictate. She must take her place with all other
created beings.

That is the essence of this rebuke. So, let us draw our
conclusions. The first is with regard to Mary herself.
She is worthy of all honour as the one to whom the
high privilege was given of being the earthly mother of
Jesus of Nazareth, the Son of God: 'Made of the seed
of David according to the flesh' (Romans 1:3). She was
the one chosen for that great honour and that great
principle: but she is only a woman. There is no suggestion whatsoever in the Bible of the immaculate conception – that Mary was born in a sinless state. That is
entire imagination. It is pure importation. It is, indeed,
a denial of what we are told here by the Son of God

himself. 'Woman!' Like everybody else, she belongs to that natural realm and our Lord is urging upon her the importance of realising that. Not only that, she is a fallible woman, a mistaken woman, a sinful woman. She needs to be rebuked by the Son of God as much as any one of us does. That is the picture we have of Mary here and throughout the New Testament.

But I want to emphasise this: if, as our Lord makes so plain and clear here, Mary could not direct and influence his conduct while he was here in the state of his humiliation, how much less can she do so now, in his state of exaltation. You know the teaching: 'Pray to Mary.' Mary gets the prominence! Why? 'Well,' it is said, 'she is nearer to us. She is more sympathetic. He is away in the distance. Ask Mary to persuade him. She has great influence over her Son and she can get him to act.'

Any such teaching is a blank contradiction of our Lord's words here. Mary has no influence upon him: What have we in common? This is my affair. Leave it to me. Do not interfere. Do not try to tell me what to do.

Our Lord acts independently of Mary here, and he still does. He needs no one to influence him on our behalf, and he will not tolerate any attempt at such influence.

Can you not see that the very suggestion that we need to pray to Mary, that she may influence him, is blasphemous? It is to derogate from his heart of love, from his sympathy, from his understanding, from his nearness to us. The very idea that we need any inter-mediary detracts from the glory of his complete divine and perfect Saviourhood.

He is still the same now as he was when he was here on earth – the tender, loving, compassionate Jesus, 'touched

with the feeling of our infirmities' (Hebrews 4:15). He
does not need intermediaries, and in his life on earth
whenever they tried to insinuate themselves they were
always rebuked. Here Mary is rebuked. The notion that
we have to pray through her and get her to intercede on
our behalf, and put in a good word, and persuade him
to do something, is, as I said, an insult to our Lord.

But lastly, and for ourselves, let us learn this lesson.
Are we not at times guilty of the same sin of presumption – the sin of going to him and dictating to him? We
rush into his presence and say, 'Grant me this, I must
have it. You're able to give this, why don't you do it?'
Is not that the sort of thing we have all been tempted to
do? Do you demand things? Do you claim things? Do
you say, 'Do this *now*'?

Our Lord rebuked his earthly mother for presumption, but must we not all plead guilty? We always want
God's blessings to come in the way and at the time we
have chosen. Like children, we are annoyed if God does
not answer the moment we ask. But the very thought
that we have the right to go to God and make demands!
Some people even demand miracles for the sake of
miracles, or for the sake of their own aggrandisement.

Here is the answer, and never let us forget this. God
is a sovereign Lord. He knows his own will. He decides
when to act and how to act. He knows what is best for
us. And everything is for his glory. Let us, therefore,
beware of this sin of presumption. We must leave ourselves in his hands.

Mary – let us say this to her honour and her credit –
saw that. Our Lord did rebuke her, and yet he did not
say, 'I am not going to do anything.' What he said was:

I am not going to do it now at your request. 'Mine hour is not yet come.' I am going to do it but I am going to do it in my time and in my way, not at your demand, not under your orders.

Our Lord refuses to do things when we want him to, when we demand that he act. But thank God that with the rebuke there is a word of comfort. Listen to how Isaiah expresses this. With prophetic vision he writes, 'And therefore will the Lord wait, that he may be gracious unto you, and therefore will he be exalted, that he may have mercy upon you: for the Lord is a God of judgment: blessed are all they that wait for him' (Isaiah 30:18). That is the lesson: 'Blessed are all they that wait for him.' You know that he has the power, he has the capacity. You want to praise him. You want to know him. You want to have the baptism of the Spirit. You want to have his love filling your heart. Are you guilty of impatience? Are you beginning to dictate? Are you demanding? If so, you are delaying the blessing. 'Blessed are all they that wait for him.' Or, as it is found in Habakkuk: 'For the vision is yet for an appointed time, but at the end it shall speak, and not lie: though it tarry, wait for it; because it will surely come, it will not tarry' (Habakkuk 2:3).

Let us therefore learn this preliminary lesson from the marriage feast at Cana of Galilee. Stop grumbling, stop nagging, stop complaining and demanding. Take the rebuke that was given to Mary. Humble yourself. Wait patiently for him. Accept Mary's advice given to the servants: 'Whatsoever he saith unto you, do it.' Simply be obedient and wait for him. 'Blessed are all they that wait for him.'

2

Trust and Obey

*And Jesus was called, and his disciples, to the marriage.
And when they wanted wine, the mother of Jesus saith
unto him, They have no wine Jesus saith unto her,
Woman, what have I to do with thee? mine hour is not
yet come. His mother saith unto the servants, Whatsoever he saith unto you, do it. And there were set there
six waterpots of stone, after the manner of the purifying
of the Jews, containing two or three firkins apiece. Jesus
saith unto them, Fill the waterpots with water. And
they filled them up to the brim. And he saith unto them,
Draw out now, and bear unto the governor of the feast.
And they bare it.* John 2:2–8

A miracle, let me remind you, is a parable; it is meant
to teach us. And I am suggesting that the great purpose
of the miracle at Cana, and of the other miracles, is to
bring us to a realisation of what has been made possible
for us through our Lord and Saviour. I am suggesting
also that the key verse of John's Gospel is this: 'And of

his fullness have all we received, and grace for grace'
(John 1:16). In a sense, the whole object of the Gospel
is to bring us to realise the nature of that fullness, and
to show us how we can receive it.

John gives explicit teaching about this, and there are
also these incidents where the teaching is implicit.

If we only observed what we are told in the stories
and miracles of John's Gospel, as well as in the teaching, we should have great understanding with regard to
the vital matter of knowing the fullness of Christ. In
these incidents we see the condescension of God and of
his dear Son. They stoop to our weakness. They know
that we are helped by illustrations and examples and so
they provide them for us in rich profusion.

So we have begun to consider this story of the wedding in Cana and we have emphasised, first, that our
Lord is always central. He dominates the whole situation as he does the history of the world. Secondly, we
asked the question: How are we to receive of the fullness
that is in him? And in the behaviour of Mary we saw
some of the dangers and pitfalls that we must avoid.
Mary falls into the sin of impatience and presumption
and she tries to dictate to him. But our Lord
reprimands her: 'Mine hour is not yet come.' Our
Lord's teaching is: I do these things in my time, in my
way.

I trust we have, therefore, learned the great lesson
that we must start with a realisation of his sovereignty.
Nothing is so fatal in the Christian life, and in the
enjoyment of this fullness, as any element of impatience. We are supplicants, not dictators. We can make
no demands. We have no rights. We deserve nothing.

We have learned that from Mary and we ended the last sermon by saying that it is vitally important that we should listen to her advice. After our Lord's rebuke this is the best thing that comes out. 'His mother saith unto the servants, Whatsoever he saith unto you, do it.' Now that is absolutely right, and that is the point we take up again. I want to emphasise this for it is not only Mary's advice, it is the advice given to us by the saints of the centuries. If you are desiring, as I am sure you are, to know and to receive more and more of Christ's fullness, what are you to do?

Let me start with a valuable piece of preliminary advice: listen to those who have trodden this path before you. This is a great lesson, much needed by modern men and women in the self-confidence and assurance they feel because they live in the twentieth century. Self-confidence is, I suppose, the greatest stumblingblock of all in the spiritual realm. Who are we? What do we know about God? What is the value of all our scientific understanding? It does not help at all. It does not make any difference in the realm of the fullness of life.

No, we must listen to those who have been in this world before us. They were men and women like ourselves. They, too, had to fight the world and the flesh and the devil. But they understood the possibilities of the Christian life. So they sought it and they struggled, and, thank God, many of them wrote their autobiographies; we also have their sermons and letters. They have told us in detail how they conducted themselves and what they did, and their words are invaluable to us.

So down the centuries there comes this advice from

the saints of all the ages. In all the communions of the church, in every country, and with one unanimous voice, they all tell us what Mary said to these servants, 'Whatsoever he saith unto you, do it.' That is the first advice that is given to us as we approach this whole great question. We come in our need. We also 'have no wine'. We are exhausted. We are at the end. We need something. What are we to do? Well, *he* is the answer, and the only answer, and this is our approach to him: 'Whatsoever he saith unto you, do it.'

Now let us analyse that. I put it, first of all, as a principle, a doctrine. We must learn at the very beginning that there are two elements in knowing God's fullness, two sides, and if we forget one or the other, we shall go astray. There is his part – that is vital – but there is our part also, and this is important. Now the danger lies in emphasising the one or the other, and emphasising the one at the expense of the other, and many go astray at this point. Probably we have all, at some time, gone astray on one side or the other.

The first danger is, of course, too much self-reliant activity, the feeling that we ourselves can achieve a state of holiness and blessing, and we set out to do this, encouraged by manuals like the *Imitation of Christ*. We assume that we have the ability and the capacity in and of ourselves, and therefore we put all our emphasis upon our side, our aspect. So we go on until we become utterly weary and exhausted – taking resolutions, trying, determining, setting out, only to get discouraged and fail. Then we start again and go through the whole process once more. That is the Christian life of so many people, and it is entirely due to the fact that the whole emphasis has been placed upon our side, upon what we must do.

And then the other danger, the exact opposite, is so to emphasise God's side as to say that we must become completely passive, that we must just wait and wait and wait, doing nothing at all.

It is fascinating to see the story of these two emphases throughout the history of the church. It has been written about many times. I suppose one of the best books, in the twentieth century at any rate, was the famous series of Bampton Lectures by Dr Kenneth E. Kirk called *The Vision of God*, in which he traces the history of these two ideas as they have battled with one another in the lives of individuals and of the church throughout the running centuries, showing us clearly the error on both sides.

So there is a danger on the one side and on the other. This is not surprising, of course, because the moment you set out to know something of the fullness of Christ or to reach the higher reaches of the spiritual life, you can be certain that the devil will redouble his efforts to hinder you. As he attacked our blessed Lord, he will attack you. He will trip you up and trap you. He will come as an angel of light and will urge you to over-activity or to a complete passivity, anything as long as he can frustrate your efforts and keep you earth-bound and lacking in the true knowledge of the fullness of Christ.

What, then, is the true position? Well, it is here in perfection in this great story. The balance that we see here is always the great characteristic of the Scriptures. It is activity under his control, or, to put it the other way round, it is his activity through us. The two are essential. 'Whatsoever he saith unto you, do it.' And we must do it. He says; we do. So we are told, 'Jesus saith unto them, Fill the waterpots with water. And they filled them up to the brim. And he saith unto them, Draw out now, and bear unto the governor of the feast. And they bare it.' The two elements are here and they are blended perfectly.

Let me therefore emphasise this: as long as we bear these two things in mind we will avoid many of the initial difficulties. The moment we realise that it is his activity through us, or our activity under his control and guidance, we will get rid of what may be called the fussiness of so much spiritual experience and activity. What a terrible thing fussiness is – in every realm! You see two people doing exactly the same job, the same work. One works quietly, calmly; the other is fussy and excited, feeling that everything depends on him or her, and the whole place is disturbed and upset.

We are exactly like that, are we not, in our spiritual lives, and it is almost entirely due to this lack of balance. We are not under his control as we should be. No, we must start by realising that all our activity in and of itself will bring us nowhere. We must start by realising our inability and our complete dependence upon his direction. That, to me, is the big thing that stands out in this incident. We have seen it negatively in the error of Mary, and the corresponding rebuke that our Lord had to administer to her. Now we are looking at it more positively, and the lesson is that we must start by submitting ourselves entirely to his way.

There is a method in these matters, a glorious method, and as long as we are fighting, as long as we are trying to insinuate a little of our own thinking, we shall always be going astray. We have our ideas about this fullness and we generally expect that the blessing will come to us in some direct, marvellous and spectacular manner. We think that, of course, because we have read of people to whom it has come like that. Then we tend to say, 'Now, this is the way!' We expect it to happen like that, and because it does not, we are in terrible trouble. We feel that we are not being dealt with fairly and begin to grumble and complain.

A lot of teaching encourages this wrong thinking. Not only are we told that the blessing must come in a spectacular way, but that it must come in a meeting. We must do this and that and it is bound to come. And then we try it and it does not come, and we are wondering what it is all about. No, all presuppositions must be dismissed. We must not bring carnal thinking into this realm. Christians can do that, in spite of the fact that at the point of justification, at the point of conversion, they had to abandon presuppositions and simply believe. Having done that, they go on, and bring their old thinking right back again into this other phase. But the Christian life is all by faith, from beginning to end.

There is a great danger of expecting something striking, spectacular, marvellous. But it does not come like that. Generally speaking these blessings come in the Christian life along the line of ordinary duty. Here it is you see: 'Fill the waterpots.' There is nothing more ordinary than that. What a menial job! Water is something that they do not even serve up. What Mary expects I do not know, but obviously it is something much more dramatic than this. But this is our Lord's way. He gives the most ordinary command: 'Fill the waterpots. And they filled them up to the brim.'

The Bible is full of illustrations of this, is it not? Let me remind you of perhaps the classic example. The prophet Elijah, a great man, a mighty man of God, was discouraged; he was grumbling and complaining. In 1 Kings 19 we read that he ran away to a cave on Mount Horeb. But God told him to come out of the cave and stand there on the side of the mountain. And then what happened? Well, there was a mighty rushing wind, majestic, smashing the rocks to pieces, but God was not in the wind. That is what Elijah was expecting – some signal demonstration on God's side, the wind and the power: 'But God was not in the wind.' That was followed by an earthquake, shaking the rocks: 'But God was not in the earthquake.' And then came a terrible, raging fire: 'But God was not in the fire.' Then: 'the still small voice'. That is it. The rebuke is implicit there. God did that quite deliberately. And we all need this rebuke. We all are looking, are we not, for the wind, the earthquake or the fire. But we find that the blessing will probably come through just 'filling the waterpots'. It is the 'still small voice'; something quiet, unexpected; something humdrum and usual.

> Sometimes a light surprises
> The Christian while he sings.
> *William Cowper*

This principle is fundamental, and if we are not clear about it at the very beginning, we shall certainly go astray. I must come down to details, but the details can be a danger unless I keep to the principle I have laid down.

Let us, then, apply all this to our receiving the fullness of Christ and see how it works out. What is our part? We must do, I repeat, what he tells us. 'Whatsoever he saith unto you, do it.' What does this mean? Well, let me translate it: it simply means keeping the commandments. Now that is extraordinary, is it not? This is where the shock always comes. We say, 'I believe that there is a marvellous experience that I can have, and I am now going to put myself into a position where this dramatic thing can take place.' And after my fuss, and bother, and excitement, and my loss of temper, and my impatience, when I have come to my senses again, the 'still small voice' comes to me and says, 'Keep the commandments.' Is not this surprising? But here it is. It is the obvious message here, as it is of the whole Bible. This must always come first.

In other words, it is useless to expect any great blessing from God if we are disobedient. It is as simple as that. We, of course, are ready to indulge in heroics. We will go to the ends of the earth. There is nothing we will not do in order to get this great, this dramatic thing. But it is of no value at all unless we keep the commandments. There are principles in the Christian life, and they cannot be violated. We are all interested in short cuts. We want things in our way. We say, 'This is the way I'd like to have it.' But you will not get it. You are wasting your energy, and you are only frustrating yourself. Heroics are of no value at all.

There is an incident that once happened in my own experience. I remember preaching in Manchester and during the service I felt that God was using and honouring the preaching. At the close of the service a very intelligent young lady came to me and said that she had seen something that she had never seen before. She said, 'Now I want to live this life. It came to me quite clearly while listening to you. Now if you, as a servant of God, tell me that I am to give up my post here in Manchester' (and she had quite a good post) 'and go and live and work in the heart of Africa, I am prepared to do it.'

'All right,' I said, 'but what if the message that I give you is that you stay here in Manchester and go on doing what you are doing – are you prepared to do that?'

And immediately her face fell. Going to Africa! Rushing to the ends of the earth! Heroics! The answer is, of course, that you may be called to do that, I am not denying it, but if you try to dictate that God's blessing must come in that way, it will not. 'Fill the waterpots.' Keep the commandments. Live the godly life where you are – exactly where you are. Some tremendous sacrifice does not count with God if we are not keeping the commandments and obeying him.

We have the authority of our Lord himself in explicit teaching on this matter of obedience. Having taught the disciples on one occasion, he rounded off his words like this: 'If ye know these things, happy are ye if ye do them' (John 13:17). You can know them, but if you want real happiness, if you want joy, if you want the real bliss of the Christian life, you must do them. 'If ye know these things, happy are ye if ye do them' – if you practise them and put them into operation.

This is so crucial that it is no use proceeding unless we are clear about it. In the fourteenth chapter of this same Gospel of John, our Lord has put it plainly and has repeated it – and it needs to be repeated! We can never hear these things too often. Listen to him: 'He that hath my commandments, and keepeth them, he it is that loveth me: and he that loveth me shall be loved of my Father, and I will love him, and will manifest myself to him' (John 14:21). Now what is our desire? Is it not to see the Son of God? He has said, 'I will manifest myself to him.' That is what we want; that is the fullness that we are seeking together. To whom does he reveal himself? The answer is that he reveals himself to those who love him. Who are those who love him? Those who are prepared to go to the heart of Africa, those who are prepared to make some striking sacrifice, some spectacular action? No, no! 'He that hath my commandments, and keepeth them, he it is that loveth me.'

But go on to verse 22: 'Judas saith unto him, not Iscariot, Lord, how is it that thou wilt manifest thyself unto us, and not unto the world?'

Here is the answer: 'Jesus answered and said unto him, If a man love me, he will keep my words' – the same thing – 'and my Father will love him, and we will come unto him, and make our abode with him.' This is what you want, is it not? You want to know that God the Father, and God the Son, and God the Holy Spirit are making their abode in you. You want to know the presence of God. This is the *summum bonum* of the Christian life and experience in this world.

'Oh, how can I get that?' asks someone.

And that is the answer: 'If a man love me, he will keep my words . . .' Then our Lord goes on in verse 24: 'He that loveth me not keepeth not my sayings: and the word which ye hear is not mine, but the Father's which sent me.'

Are we clear about this – about the necessity of keeping the commandments, doing whatsoever he tells us? 'Fill the waterpots.' What does this mean, then, in practice? It means that we give a wholehearted obedience, in detail, to the commandments of God. Mary very rightly puts her emphasis on the word *whatsoever*. The danger is to obey God's commandments in general. We must obey in detail. It is as simple as that. I am not only drawing on the biblical teaching here but also on the testimony and advice given to us by the saints of the centuries. This is Mary's advice, and they have all repeated it: 'Whatsoever he saith unto you, do it,' in every single detail. It is no use claiming to take on the whole of the Christian life, and then playing with details, or not troubling even to know anything about them. There are no short cuts in the Christian life, none whatsoever.

The apostle Paul says to Timothy, 'And if a man also strive for masteries, yet is he not crowned, except he strive lawfully' (2 Timothy 2:5). What does that mean? Well, Paul has a picture of a race, a racecourse. There are the posts, and you must run on the outside of those posts. A runner is very anxious to win the prize, and there he is running. He suddenly thinks to himself, 'If I cut in there I will gain on my opponent.' So he does, and round he goes and cuts in again. He thinks he is so clever and he demands the prize. But he has forgotten the umpire! '. . . except he strive lawfully.' There are rules, regulations, laws, which must be observed in particular, and, 'All things are naked and opened unto the eyes of him with whom we have to do' (Hebrews 4:13).

I think that anybody, of any age whatsoever, in the Christian life, will agree with what I am saying. It is in the outworking of the details that we tend to fail. Take the illustration of a machine, or a car. You may think that that little screw or bolt on your vehicle does not matter. It is such a small screw and so insignificant and you do not take the trouble to screw it in tightly. You finish the job quickly and off you go, leaving behind that other man, that poor fool who takes such time to get everything right! So you drive along the road but suddenly your car stops – the screws count, everything counts. And it is like that in the whole of the spiritual life.

Do you want to know God? Do you want to know that the Father and the Son have taken up their abode in you? Do you want to receive of his fullness, and receive grace upon grace? Do you want to know something of the mountain top of the spiritual life? Here is the way to get there. You do not send for an aeroplane or a helicopter, you must start walking and climbing up. It is the only way. You must listen to the commandments in detail.

What are they? Well, here is one of them – read the Bible and study it. I mean the whole book, not snippets, not 'digests' of the Bible. I do not mean just little portions. I do not mean taking somebody else's thoughts. I mean really reading it and studying it. I mean praying as you read that the Holy Spirit will enlighten you.

Now again, when we consult those who have gone before us, we find that they are unanimous in their testimony about this. There has never been a great saint but that he or she has been a great reader of the Bible, a keen student of it, one who revels in it, has searched it and has concentrated upon its detailed teaching. It is essential. The more one reads this book and studies it, the more marvellous it becomes and the more one is amazed at one's own ignorance – how one has missed this and has not observed that. The more you give yourself to it, the sooner you will experience this blessing which you covet and for which you long.

What else? Well, of course, prayer. Prayer is seeking the face of God. Look at the time our blessed Lord himself spent in prayer, communing with God the Father. Prayer is absolutely essential. There has never been a saint but that he or she has known what it is to pray and to pray frequently. I am not emphasising so much the length of your prayers as the frequency. As one old Puritan put it, 'Keep short accounts with God.' If you desire to know that he is dwelling in you, then seek him, speak to him. Rush to him often, as you rush to someone whom you love. Keep in his presence; cultivate it. Keep yourself in the love of God. Keep near to him. Keep speaking to him.

Now this, again, seems so ordinary, does it not, as if to say that anybody can read the Bible, anybody can pray? Can they? I wonder how many of us do read the Bible? How many of us truly pray? You do not have to rush here and there, or indulge in heroics or look for some kind of package. No, this is the way: keep the commandments. He has given you his word – read it.

He has made the way open to you as a Christian to enter into his presence, so, tread along it, get there, seek him. 'Enter into the holiest by the blood of Jesus' (Hebrews 10:19). Do not sit down and mope or try to follow techniques that help other people. Go directly to him; seek him; speak to him; tell him what you want; lay yourself open to his blessed word of encouragement and of cheer and of commandment.

And then, in addition to Bible reading and prayer, seek the fellowship of his people. This has been a great means of blessing throughout the centuries. 'For none of us liveth to himself, and no man dieth to himself' (Romans 14:7), and none of us gets a real blessing on our own. Blessings have come to God's people when they have been assembled together. God looks down upon them and he gives them a common blessing which helps all of them, and it helps us all to talk together about these things.

One of the highlights in John Bunyan's autobiography, *Grace Abounding*, is a passage in which he describes a time in his life when he was trying to live the Christian life entirely by his own hard work. One day he was walking through one of the streets of Bedford, when he happened to see three or four poor women sitting together outside a door in the sun. Bunyan began to listen to them and found they were talking together about the blessings of the Christian life. They were talking of a life of peace and joy and love through faith in Jesus, of which the great John Bunyan at that time knew nothing. And as they talked they were being helped and built up. So the blessing was increased and, without knowing it, they were

blessing poor John Bunyan who went away determined
to discover for himself the life of which they spoke.

You will read in the Old Testament prophets that
when an age was evil, when it was godless, like our
present age, then the word of God was precious, and
the people of God met together frequently. 'Then they
that feared the Lord spake often one to another'
(Malachi 3:16). To talk about these things is one of the
greatest blessings that one can ever have in this life and
it leads to yet greater blessing.

And then, of course, I need scarcely say that in addition to doing all this, we now come to the realm of
practical conduct and behaviour. Here is the rub, is it
not? It is one thing to feel God's blessing in the house
of God, but the real test comes in the midst of life. 'Fill
the waterpots' – a menial task! Oh yes, in our life in the
home, in the office, the shop, the university, the
factory, here the question is: Are we keeping the
commandments?

Again, I could quote to you almost endlessly on this
matter. Listen to Paul: 'Holding the mystery of the faith
in a pure conscience' (1 Timothy 3:9). 'The mystery of
the faith': here is the jewel, here is the gem. It is such a
wonderful, such a precious thing. We have got to carry it
and we must hold it and protect it in the right casket.
And what is this casket? Well, says Paul, the only thing
that is worthy of being a casket for this 'mystery of the
faith' is a 'pure conscience'. These things cannot be
separated. The mystery, the marvel, the wonder! Ah
yes, but it is indissolubly tied to 'a pure conscience', a
'conscience void of offence' (Acts 24:16).

Or take the way John puts it in his first Epistle: 'If

we say that we have fellowship with him, and walk in darkness, we lie, and do not the truth' (1 John 1:6). Here is something that is completely impossible: we cannot walk with him in the light, and have fellowship with him in the light, and be walking in darkness at the same time; it just cannot be done. You may be a genius – we all think we are, of course! You are clever and you are going to get all these blessings, but you cannot if you are in darkness. You are wasting your time and energy. You cannot walk in the light and in the darkness at the same time, your legs are too short! It cannot be done. Give it up. Do not be a fool.

But John goes further, using very strong language: 'He that saith, I know him, and keepeth not his commandments, is a liar, and the truth is not in him' (1 John 2:4).

What a book this Bible is! That is what it says to many of us. You say, 'I am seeking this fullness but God is not answering my prayer. I have not had this blessing.' And do you know what John says to you? You are a liar. You are not honest. You say that you know him, and want to know him better, but you are not keeping his commandments. It is no use talking about your great love for him if you are not obeying him. The one who keeps his commandments is the one who really loves him. John says: Out upon this suggestion! You are a barefaced liar! Look at yourself in a mirror, and then get down on your knees in penitence and contrition, and ask him to have mercy upon you.

Or, finally, listen to Paul writing to Titus: 'This is a faithful saying, and these things I will that thou affirm constantly, that they which have believed in God might be careful to maintain good works' (Titus 3:8). Very ordinary, is it not? 'Fill the waterpots.' 'Be careful to maintain good works.' There is no by-passing the commandments. They are the commandments of God, and Christ did not come into this world to do away with them. He came to fulfil them and to enable us to fulfil them. He was made 'an offering for sin' (Isaiah 53:10). He came, '. . . in the likeness of sinful flesh, and for sin . . . That the righteousness of the law might be fulfilled in us, who walk not after the flesh, but after the Spirit' (Romans 8:3–4).

So we must keep the commandments. But we come now to the second element in this command, and that is 'filling the waterpots'. What does this represent? Now here we move into a realm that is even beyond obedience to the commandments. Obedience is basic and there must be no argument about that. Obedience presupposes everything else. If I am not doing my utmost to keep the commandments, then I have no right to listen to this next point. But if I am clear that I must keep them, and maintain good works and observe his word, then he leads me a step higher: 'Fill the waterpots.'

Now the instruction to fill the waterpots is a big leap, is it not? Mary has said, 'They have no wine.' The need is for wine. But our Lord says, 'Fill the waterpots with water.' If he had given us some extraordinary and marvellous commandment, we would do it, but he talks about water and waterpots.

We are moving into the realm of faith now. There is an element here of venturing, of trusting. A man or woman who is a Christian and who can read at all intelligently sees the commandment, there is no need for much faith about that. I call that commonsense. But here is a step beyond that – 'Fill the waterpots with *water.*' This does not seem to have much relevance to the problem of the need for wine, does it? But that is what our Lord says. And the command is, 'Whatsoever he saith unto you, do it.'

Now this is the point at which, having seen the truth about the way of salvation, and having become Christians, and having seen that we are to keep the commandments in all things, we come to the realisation of the great possibilities of the Christian life. We nearly all start, do we not, by thinking of the Christian life mainly in terms of forgiveness of sins. We have been convicted of sin and we do not want to go to hell, so we believe the gospel teaching that Christ died for us and we are saved. Now we are saved, all is well.

Not at all! We come to a point when we begin to realise that that is only the beginning of Christianity, that Christianity means this: 'Of his fulness have all we received, and grace for [upon] grace' (John 1:16). Or, as Paul says, that we 'may be able to comprehend with all saints what is the breadth, and length, and depth, and height; and to know the love of Christ, which passeth knowledge, that ye might be filled with all the fulness of God' (Ephesians 3:18–19). We begin to realise that that is possible in this life, in this world.

Peter says, 'having escaped the corruption that is in the world through lust'. That is the negative, but the positive is this: 'Whereby are given unto us exceeding great and precious promises: that by these ye might become partakers of the divine nature . . .' (2 Peter 1:4).

Our eyes are opened. We are now entering the realm of the supernatural and the miraculous – the realm of the 'exceeding great and precious promises'. We begin to see the possibilities to the Christian in this life and world.

At first, of course, we are staggered. We hear his commandment, his voice saying, 'Do this, begin to enter here, "Fill the waterpots with water,"' and we do not understand it. Flesh cringes, shrinks from it, it seems impossible. Is this ecstasy? What is this? Is it really something actual? Is it not just hyperbole? Is it not some poetic description? 'All the fulness of God' – yes, but is that practical? Is that something I can really know and experience? Do these things actually happen?

These are the questions that immediately flash across our minds. But here is the vital point: 'Whatsoever he saith unto you, do it.' 'Fill the waterpots with water,' which means just this: that we believe in this blessed, glorious possibility simply and solely because it is he who has told us about it. It is his promise, not ours. It is there. It is written. He has said it. He says 'Do.' And without understanding, without knowing, I do. I believe that it is possible for me to know the living God in a real manner, to have real communion with Christ in this life and to know something of all this fullness of God. That is the next step.

And then the final step is the drawing of the water. This is much more difficult. 'Fill the waterpots with water. And they filled them up to the brim.' The pots were there, as they had always been, in connection with the purification, the ritual washing of hands. Then listen: 'And he saith unto them, Draw out now, and bear unto the governor of the feast.' In effect, our Lord is saying, 'You have filled those waterpots with water – all right. Draw the wine out of them now.' But what is he talking about? We have just put water in and he says, 'Draw the wine out'!

Here is the crucial moment. It is the crucial moment in every miracle. We see a perfect illustration in another miracle in the Gospels. One Sabbath our Lord was in the synagogue when he saw a man with a withered hand. Here was a man who could not move his hand – it was withered, paralysed, the muscles had atrophied. And our Lord said to him, 'Stretch forth thine hand.' This is divine humour. This is the marvel, the paradox of Christianity. This is the glory of it. And that is why it is the only hope today, for this evil old world and many a hopeless, rotten soul. There is infinite hope for you.

Why? Because we have a Saviour who does things like this. He sees a man with a withered hand and says, 'Stretch forth thine hand.' But that is the one thing the man cannot do! Our Lord tells him to do what is impossible. Yet Mark writes, 'And he stretched it out: and his hand was restored whole as the other' (Mark 3:1–5). He commands and as he commands, he gives the power. He enables us to do what is impossible: 'Draw out now, and bear unto the governor of the feast. And they bare it.' And that is the measure of their faith.

Now this is a vital element in the whole matter of seeking his fullness: keep the commandments, realise the possibilities, the precious promises, and when he speaks – act!

> He speaks, and listening to His voice
> New life the dead receive.
> *Charles Wesley*

What does it mean? Well here it is:

> Trust and obey!
> For there's no other way
> To be happy in Jesus –
> But to trust and obey.
> *J. H. Sammis*

> Venture on Him, venture only,
> Let no other trust intrude.
> *Joseph Hart*

This principle is given to us in pictorial manner in this first miracle, this first sign, performed in Cana of Galilee, in which our Lord reveals something of his glory so that his disciples believe in a new and in a greater manner. And the principles governing the receiving of his fullness are still precisely the same.

3

The Nature of the Blessing

Jesus saith unto them, Fill the waterpots with water. And they filled them up to the brim. And he saith unto them, Draw out now, and bear unto the governor of the feast. And they bare it. When the ruler of the feast had tasted the water that was made wine, and knew not whence it was: (but the servants which drew the water knew;) the governor of the feast called the bridegroom, and saith unto him, Every man at the beginning doth set forth good wine; and when men have well drunk, then that which is worse: but thou hast kept the good wine until now.

[Then the summing up:] This beginning of miracles did Jesus in Cana of Galilee, and manifested forth his glory; and his disciples believed on him. John 2:7–11

We have seen that nothing is more important than that we should know how we can receive of his fullness, and here, thank God, in the account of this first sign or miracle, a great deal of instruction is given us. There are many pitfalls, we are surrounded by difficulties, and

53

our great adversary the devil would ever lead us astray. He even transforms himself into an angel of light and twists the Scriptures in order to hinder us, as he has hindered all God's saints. Therefore, it is vitally important for us to discover the rules, the principles, which govern this whole matter, and I am suggesting that in the miracle of the water turned into wine we are given valuable instruction.

There is a hymn which goes:

> Jesus, the very thought of Thee
> With sweetness fills the breast.
> *Bernard of Clairvaux*

Those words are an expression of true Christianity. Bernard of Clairvaux was describing his experience when he wrote this hymn, and according to the New Testament, the words express the position that we all should be in. But are they true of us? Do they describe our experience? We should not merely hold these things with our intellects – that is not Christianity. True Christianity is a life, a whole life and a full life. And it is, of course, a life that is especially related to him: 'Of his fulness have all we received, and grace upon grace.' It is an expanding, growing, continuing, increasing life.

I am calling attention to this, not only that we might enjoy these great benefits for which the Son of God died on a cruel cross, but for a further reason. As the history of the church demonstrates so clearly to us, it is when Christian people are manifesting this quality of life in their daily living that the world is arrested and apprehended. That is ultimately the means of evangelism, though I do not wish to say, of course, that we must do nothing else.

The tragedy today, it seems to me, is that so many assume that the church is all right and that all we need to do is think up methods which will attract the outsider. But it is by this abundant life in us that we attract outsiders, for they are living next door to us, or working at the next desk in the office, or they are fellow students or in the same profession. It is as they see the love and life of our Lord in us that they are arrested. That is how Christianity spread at the beginning; that is how it spread in the Reformation and in all periods of revival in the long story of the church.

So what could be more important than receiving the fullness that our Lord gives? And in the wedding at Cana, in this picture that is set before us, it is easy to apprehend some of the great principles for receiving the fullness. We have already learned a number of them through Mary. We have learned what we must not do. We must not dictate, but must submit utterly to our Lord and realise that he is the sovereign Lord in these matters.

If we have not learned this first principle, there is no point in going on. If there is a restless over-anxiety in your spirit, or almost a complaint, then you might as well give up; it is no good. This fullness is a gift of God and we must obey the injunction that Mary gave to these servants: 'Whatsoever he saith unto you, do it.' We must 'trust and obey'. The fact that we are seeking his sovereign gift does not mean we enter into a negative passivity. No, no! We can be passive and active at the same time.

So do we believe that if we are disobedient, or rebellious, it is no use craving some unusual blessing? Do we realise that to trust and obey is the high road to blessing, that this is his method? The Bible is always consistent, and the ultimate end and object of it all is to bring us to perfection. God is concerned about our sanctification, our holiness. Forgiveness is not the end, escaping hell is not the objective. His purpose is for us to be 'conformed to the image of his Son' (Romans 8:29).

There, then, is our side of it, but let us move on to what is much more important – our Lord's side, our Lord's part, and this, of course, is everything. As I have pointed out, the thing that strikes us in the account of the miracle at Cana is his presence. He dominates the whole situation. Why? Because the power is in him. 'He manifested forth his glory' (verse 11), and in that glory there is this power. It is the glory of the deity, the glory of the Godhead. He is the eternal Son of God, and here he reveals something of his omnipotence, his everlasting power.

It is, of course, a uniquely Christian emphasis that all blessings are in our Lord Jesus Christ. We are not interested in a teaching or theory or rule of life which may be very good in and of itself, and may even say a lot about God the Father. If it does not include Christ and make him central, we are not interested, it is not Christianity. That people believe in God or do good does not make them Christians. As the apostle Paul writes, 'That their hearts might be comforted, being knit together in love, and unto all riches of the full assurance of understanding, to the acknowledgement of the mystery of God, and of the Father, and of

Christ; in whom are hid all the treasures of wisdom and knowledge' (Colossians 2:2–3).

The New Testament expresses the centrality of Christ in endless ways. One of the commonest, perhaps, is to refer to him as the Head of the church, using the figure of a body (Ephesians 4:15–16), and the head, of course, is the seat of all power, of all the nervous energy. It is all there in the head, in the brain, and the rest of the body is dependent upon that. The fullness, the power, the life, all comes out from Christ, our great Head, and then permeates through the remainder of the body. But the emphasis is, of course, that he is the Head of 'all principality and power' (Colossians 2:10), that he is the Head of the church, and all blessings, all power, everything comes to us in him and through him and from him.

Therefore, as these people at the marriage feast of Cana of Galilee reached the point at which they were utterly and solely dependent upon his ability, so are we. And this is one of the first things that we must realise.

Now the history of the church on the subject of depending on God is fascinating. In many ways, one of the greatest snares at this point is the snare of what is called *mysticism*. Mysticism can be put roughly like this: it is 'seeking the God that is in you'. It says that the Spirit of God is in all people, and therefore we must look into ourselves and surrender to the Spirit of God that is within. The mystics instruct us how to do that. They tell us the various steps and stages of the 'mystic way', which leads ultimately to the 'beatific vision'.

But mysticism can be a snare and danger, and often

has been, because so often mystics have relied upon their method, and have entirely bypassed the Lord Jesus Christ. Mysticism is always in danger of forgetting him. You see that in modern Quakerism – the Society of Friends – and their teaching. That almost invariably happens whenever there is an emphasis on 'the inner life'.

Mysticism is no use because all we need is concentrated in him. There he is, seated like the others at the feast, but the energy and the power to deal with the situation is entirely and exclusively in him. And, of course, that is in many ways the great theme of this Gospel according to John. Our Lord himself said this many times, but never more clearly than in his words, 'I am come that they might have life, and that they might have it more abundantly' (John 10:10). He did not come primarily to instruct us, but to give us life. 'In him was life,' writes John (John 1:4), and he came to enable us to partake of that life that is in him.

So look at this marriage feast again. There he is with the other guests. All the power is concentrated in him, and what matters is what he does and what he is able to do. Now that is the great lesson that we must learn.

Throughout the New Testament we are taught the all-importance and centrality of having a living relationship with him. For it is only from him that we can receive this blessed fullness. And, thank God, the emphasis is that he is always able to do this because 'with God nothing shall be impossible' (Luke 1:37). Our hymns are full of this:

> He speaks, and listening to His voice,
> New life the dead receive.
>
> *Charles Wesley*

That is the need of the whole of humanity, which is by nature 'dead in trespasses and sins' (Ephesians 2:1). We need life and he is able to give it. He says, 'Fill the waterpots with water . . . Draw out.'

Before we look at how this works out in practice, let me sum up the two sides – his part and our part. I think it is summarised perfectly in 2 Corinthians 3:18: 'We all, with open face beholding as in a glass the glory of the Lord, are being changed into the same image from glory to glory, even as by the Spirit of the Lord.'

First: 'We all, beholding . . .' That is something we go on doing. That is filling the waterpots. That is the drawing of the water. 'Beholding' is our activity. If we do not behold, nothing will happen to us. Behold means to look upon, gaze upon, set our eyes steadfastly upon. And we are to go on doing it. '. . . beholding as in a glass the glory of the Lord . . .' We look for him, as Mary had the sense to do after her initial blunder, and as these others did. We look to him. We realise that the power, the life and the glory are all in him, and we must keep our attention upon him and be responsive to him. This is activity: 'Beholding as in a glass the glory of the Lord . . .'

Then, second, as we look, this is what happens: we are being changed. We do not change ourselves. He changes us. As it is put here – we 'are changed into the same image from glory to glory, even as by the Spirit of the Lord'. It is his Spirit alone that can do this for us.

It is as we look, as we keep our gaze upon him, that he changes us 'from glory to glory', and on and on the process goes.

We find this teaching put in almost the same way in Philippians 2:12–13: 'Work out your own salvation with fear and trembling. For it is God which worketh in you both to will and to do of his good pleasure.' We work out; he works in! 'Fill the waterpots . . . Draw out now.' And even while we are filling the pots, he is working the miracle.

So we have emphasised these relative activities: the activity of the believer; the activity of the Lord, the Saviour. But now let us go on and have a look at the nature of the blessing. This, of course, is again something that is most wonderful for us. There is nothing more encouraging, nothing more stimulating. What you and I must realise, first and foremost, is what is possible to us and for us. It is an amazing thing, but it is possible for us to be Christians and to read our New Testament diligently and regularly, and miss this. Is not that the trouble with the church throughout the centuries – the failure to realise what is possible for us?

The New Testament Epistles are full of reminders and teaching about this. Take, for instance, the great Epistle to the Ephesians. The apostle Paul has been reminding the Christians in Ephesus of what has happened to them and where they are and what they are. Then, in the third chapter, he tells them that he is praying for them. He says, 'I bow my knees unto the Father of our Lord Jesus Christ.' He prays with great urgency and intensity for these people who are already believers and have the seal of the Spirit upon them. What is it that he prays? Oh, that they 'may be able to comprehend with all saints what is the breadth, and length, and depth, and height; and to know the love of Christ, which passeth knowledge, that ye might be filled with all the fulness of God' (Ephesians 3:14, 18–19). He says: You do not realise that. I want you to, and I am reminding you. He says it also in the first chapter: 'The eyes of your understanding being enlightened; that ye may know' – what? – 'what is the hope of his calling, and what the riches of the glory of his inheritance in the saints, and what is the exceeding greatness of his power to us-ward who believe' (Ephesians 1:18–19).

We live as paupers. Why? Well, very largely because we do not know our inheritance. We are not meant to live like that. We are meant to live as princes, and to enjoy this great wealth that he has come to make available – 'the unsearchable riches of Christ' (Ephesians 3:8). The fact that we do not know that is very largely because of a kind of initial difficulty in apprehending that this is meant for us, that it is true for us, that the New Testament is as applicable to us today as it was to the first-century Christian.

I notice a tendency, a teaching, creeping in at the present time which seems to cut out most of the New Testament. People say, 'Do not take too much from the book of Acts, it was only for the first Christians.' And then, of course, they are bound to say the same about the Epistles, for they were written to the first Christians and assume knowledge of the book of Acts. And thus the Spirit is being quenched because men and women are told that they already have everything they can ever receive, and all they must do is to go on quietly surrendering themselves. That seems to me to be a negation of the whole of the New Testament teaching. Let me show you what I mean.

What is the nature of this blessing that God promises us? Let me divide it up according to what we are told in this illustration of the wedding at Cana, under two main headings. Let us look for a moment at the *general character* of the blessing. The first thing that we must emphasise is that it is *miraculous*. We are told, 'This beginning of miracles [signs] did Jesus in Cana.' And that, as I have reminded you already, means the action of God. It is God alone who can work a miracle. As what happened in Cana of Galilee was a miracle, so entering into and receiving of his fullness is a miracle; it is nothing less. To understand this is vital. It is of the essence of the biblical teaching on fullness that it is entirely supernatural, entirely the result of the activity of God. 'I am not ashamed of the gospel of Christ,' says Paul to the Romans. Why not? 'For it is the power of God unto salvation to every one that believeth' (Romans 1:16). 'Christ,' Paul says to the Corinthians, 'the power of God, and the wisdom of God' (1 Corinthians 1:24).

The Christian is not a person who absorbs a Christian philosophy or a certain amount of our Lord's teaching. That is not Christianity. People can do that who are just natural unchanged men and women, men and women who belong, as it were, to Adam. That is quite feasible; it has often happened. People have often borrowed the Christian ethic and the Christian teaching, but that does not make them Christians. What makes people Christians is that God has worked a miracle in them, and it is nothing less than a new creation. It is a new birth; it is the giving of a new life: these are the terms that are used. 'You hath he quickened, who were dead . . .' wrote the apostle Paul in Ephesians 2:1. That is the difference between those who are not Christians and those who are. It is the difference between a person who is spiritually dead and one who is spiritually alive.

No human being can ever produce life: it is impossible. God alone is the author of life. And that is why I am emphasising the miraculous character of the blessing that is offered to us in Christ Jesus. We are not promised that we shall be better men and women, but that we shall be *new* men and women, that we shall be entirely different.

What is Christianity? Well, let us use the famous title of the old book by Henry Scougal: it is *The Life of God in the Soul of Man*. Once more I commend the historical approach to you. What really led to the great Evangelical Awakening in the eighteenth century, its ultimate source, was the reading of Henry Scougal's book by George Whitefield and John and Charles Wesley – that was the thing that first disturbed them. They had been brought up in the church, brought up as Christians, but they were troubled by their consciences. They tried to live a better life, tried to be more moral, indeed, tried to do a lot of good, but they could not find satisfaction. And they did not know what was wrong, even though they were not only Christians, and not only read the Bible, but were Bible students, in the process of being trained for the ministry. It was the reading of that book by old Henry Scougal, who had lived in Scotland in the previous century, that set them on the road to their receiving this great fullness, and to their amazing, unparalleled usefulness.

The whole point of Scougal's book is that Christianity is not merely the application of Christian teaching, it is not merely a higher morality which people adopt and strain to put into practice, but is essentially the working of a miracle in the soul. It is the act of God. It is God putting his own life into the souls of men. And John and Charles Wesley were at once aware that they knew nothing about this, that they had not got it. They were good men, religious men, they even fasted. They went out of their way to do good, and suffered scorn and ridicule. But no, it did not matter, they knew that they had not got this life inside them. They had not become 'partakers of the divine nature'. This was something entirely strange to them, they had never even thought of it. They said in effect, 'We've been doing this and that and it leads us to nothing. We see now that essentially Christianity is something God does to us. It is the implanting of this seed of divine life within us.'

So in the marriage feast of Cana of Galilee we see that the situation is transformed by the supernatural action of our Lord. He acts; he does something. It is a creative action. Let me put it in that great statement of the apostle Paul: 'For God, who commanded the light to shine out of darkness, hath shined in our hearts, to give the light of the knowledge of the glory of God in the face of Jesus Christ' (2 Corinthians 4:6). You see Paul's comparison? He says in effect, 'What has happened to me is comparable to what happened at the original creation. It is God commanding light to shine forth in darkness. And he has done that to me, in my heart.'

Or take 2 Corinthians 3:2-3 where Paul says, 'Ye are our epistle written in our hearts, known and read of all men: forasmuch as ye are manifestly declared to be the epistle of Christ ministered by us, written not with ink, but with the Spirit of the living God; not in tables of stone, but in fleshy tables of the heart.'

True Christianity is the action of the Spirit of God writing a new name in our hearts, doing something within the depths of the personality. The apostle uses a very important comparison, one that is needed today as it was needed then. He contrasts the position of a Jew under the Old Testament dispensation with the Ten Commandments engraved on stone. That is the letter; this is the spirit. This is altogether different. It is a writing on the fleshy tables of the heart, and nobody can do this but the Spirit of God. Paul says that he had not done it – it was merely 'ministered by us'. He was the instrument, but it was not his writing, it was not his work. The only one who can perform this work is the Holy Spirit of God sent by Christ. The power is in him. And he does it by this act of new creation, by the implantation of the seed of divine life down in the very depths of the soul and spirit and being of each one of us.

Now that is what we are reminded of here. It is not that something is put into the water which makes it nice and tasty! No, there is a radical operation! There is a change, and it is miraculous. And, of course, every Christian is a miracle. To bring anybody from death to life is a miracle. And that is exactly what happens to us all spiritually when we become truly Christian. 'You hath he quickened . . . together with Christ . . . and hath raised us up' (Ephesians 2:1, 5-6).

That, then, is the first great point, and the second is the *suddenness* with which the miracle happens. Now do not misunderstand this. I shall emphasise that it is also a process, and a gradual one, but I start with the suddenness. And I must do this, not only because I must be true to the incident which we are analysing, but because I must be true to the principle taught in this connection in the whole of the New Testament. To emphasise this is the only way to put ourselves in a safe position over and against the process outlined in the manuals of devotion and taught by the mystics and the Roman Catholic Church, and by others who follow them. We must keep distinct and discrete the fact that it is his action, that it is a miraculous action, and, therefore, can happen in a flash, 'in the twinkling of an eye' (1 Corinthians 15:52). We read, 'Draw out now, and bear unto the governor of the feast. And they bare it.' But the miracle has already happened. And we must never lose sight of this aspect of the Christian life and of receiving his fullness.

Let me illustrate what I mean. We see this so often in the accounts that many have left to us of how they entered into the knowledge of Christ and received of his fullness. We find that with a strange regularity and constancy men and women were disturbed. As we have seen with John Bunyan, John and Charles Wesley and George Whitefield, they saw that something was wrong. They began to be dissatisfied with the Christian life they had been living. They said, 'When I really look at the New Testament and then at myself or when I sing those hymns, I see the disparity. When I stop and think about what I am singing, I know the words are not true of me and I am being a hypocrite. I am not singing my own experience.' So they began to seek and to search, and sometimes went on doing so for a long time, but nothing seemed to happen. Then almost without exception they said that suddenly everything became clear to them. Something happened within them, something was done to them. And out of the darkness and the despair, and the sense of hopelessness and futility, they obtained great joy and peace.

Now I could spend the rest of this sermon and many more sermons in giving you examples of this. Remember, I am not talking about conversion, but about Christian people living under the law who are suddenly lifted to another level, and go on living on the mountain tops of the Christian life and the Christian faith. I am just trying to show what is possible to us as Christians. The tragedy is that so many of us, having entered on the Christian life, remain content with forgiveness and the first beginnings, and live a kind of moral life using Christian terminology. But it is a life of failure and frustration, lacking this great power and principle of assurance that characterises New Testament Christians.

I am not confining what I say solely to the realm of individual experience. When we look out at the Christian church as a whole, our only comfort and consolation comes here, in our knowledge that God can act in a sudden, miraculous way. Here again the testimony of history is of inestimable value. In one sense, the whole story of the church can be described as a series of pentecosts – I mean by that, a series of revivals. Here is the picture at the beginning: we see the believers together in the upper room, waiting, praying, pleading. 'Suddenly there came a sound from heaven as of a rushing mighty wind' (Acts 2:2). Suddenly!

But as we go on in the history of the church, we find that that lasts for a while, then begins to wane and down the church goes into a dull trough. Then some people are disturbed and awakened and begin to seek and to pray and to plead with God, and they may do so for years and nothing happens. But suddenly, and often unexpectedly, the Spirit is poured forth upon them. That is what we mean by revival – the descent of the Holy Spirit upon a number of God's people together, and the whole situation is transformed, exactly as it was in Cana of Galilee. He has acted.

So we are bound to emphasise this suddenness, and as I said, it is here that one is filled with a sense of hope for the Christian church. If revival were always and invariably a gradual process of development and of increase, then at the present moment I would be filled with a sense of despair, for things are not getting better but worse. But because of this principle, one is not daunted at all. He seems to withdraw himself, things go down and down and down, until the church appears to be finished, but when all seems completely hopeless, he arises, he speaks: 'Draw out the water.' And they draw out, and find that it is perfect wine. That is how it has always happened.

But that does not mean, let me remind you again, that we therefore do nothing and sink into a state of passivity. No, no! 'Fill the waterpots . . . and they filled them up to the brim.' Do everything he tells you. Do not leave anything undone. Act with all your might.

Fulfil all the conditions. But remember, the power is his. It is miraculous. It can happen at any moment – suddenly, when least expected.

Here is the hope for every one of us. As you hear my words you may be almost at the point of despair. Perhaps you have felt a dissatisfaction with the quality of your Christian life – even for years – and have been doing this and that and praying. 'But,' you say, 'nothing happens. Is it all hopeless?'

My answer to you is this: No! At any moment, when you least expect it, he will come.

> Sometimes a light surprises
> > The Christian while he sings;
> It is the Lord who rises
> > With healing in His wings.
> > > *William Cowper*

Because the power is God's power, because to act is his prerogative, he can give his blessing whenever he likes, at any moment, in spite of the conditions, as it were. He demands them and you and I must keep them but he is not tied to them. He can work in his own sovereign manner at any moment. He has done it in the history of the church and in the history of individuals. He will act in the life of every individual who does whatsoever he says and who waits in faith upon him.

But let me come to the last point, which is the *secret* aspect – and this is something very wonderful. Did you notice this? 'When the ruler of the feast had tasted the water that was made wine, and knew not whence it was: (but the servants which drew the water knew;) the governor of the feast called the bridegroom, and saith unto him, Every man at the beginning doth set forth good wine; and when men have well drunk, then that which is worse: but thou hast kept the good wine until now.'

The 'ruler', that is, the chief steward, of the feast, had been at many similar feasts. He was amazed and did not understand. He said: This is extraordinary. I've never seen anything like this before. 'But the servants which drew the water knew.' This is the secret aspect of this whole matter and it is tremendously important. Ultimately, this amazement, this incomprehension, that comes to us from others, is the proof of whether or not we have the life of God in our souls.

Are we not told that everywhere in the Acts of the Apostles? When the Holy Spirit descended upon the first believers in the upper room, on the morning of the Day of Pentecost, the whole populace marvelled. They asked, 'What meaneth this?' (Acts 2:7–12). They did not understand. The authorities in the Sanhedrin looked at Peter and John and, observing that they were unlearned and ignorant men, marvelled (Acts 4:13). They, too, did not understand it.

It is always like that. 'The natural man receiveth not the things of the Spirit of God: for they are foolishness unto him,' says Paul: 'neither can he know them, because they are spiritually discerned' (1 Corinthians 2:14). And then he says, 'But he that is spiritual judgeth all things, yet he himself is judged of no man' (verse 15). The man who has the Spirit of God in him is a man who has understanding. He apprehends and knows – as the servants who draw the water know. He understands all things, yet he himself is not understood by those without the Spirit of God.

The 'natural man' does not understand the gospel and he does not understand the Christian because something has happened to the Christian that is beyond explanation. It is miraculous. And that is why 'the wise and prudent' (Matthew 11:25) are always rejecting this gospel – it is because they want to understand it. Fools that they are! Who can understand a miracle? Of course they do not understand it.

And you should not be surprised that the clever people in the world today are denying the gospel. The philosophers and scientists are blind. Being natural men and women, they cannot understand miracles. They cannot understand any more than the master of the feast can understand here in the marriage in Cana of Galilee. But the ignoramuses, the servants, they know. They are with him. They see it happening. Ultimately they do not understand it but they know it has happened, they know it is the Lord. They have an explanation.

People may be unlearned, they may be ignorant, but if this has happened to them, they know. 'He that is spiritual judgeth all things, yet he himself is judged of no man' (1 Corinthians 3:15). He becomes an enigma, a problem, a puzzle, to everybody who is not a Christian. And this is what you and I are meant to be. We are meant to be such people that the world in which we live does not understand us. It should be amazed at us. It should say, 'What's the secret of this?' This is something that is beyond understanding, and it is not – and never is – the result of a rational process of reasoning. It is independent of reason. It is in a higher realm, beyond reason. It is not arrived at as the result of study of meditation. It is the action of God in the souls of men and women giving them the mind of Christ, giving them understanding.

Let me, finally, give you a quotation which perfectly illustrates all this. It is from Cotton Mather, a brilliant, learned man who lived in America at the end of the seventeenth and the early part of the eighteenth centuries. His academic record proves that he was a genius in every way, but listen to what he tells us. He writes that he longed to know God's rest and peace. He wanted to know of a surety that he was saved. He wanted a full assurance of his acceptance with God and of his salvation. He believed it all. He had been brought up to believe it. He had been trained as a theological student to believe it. He knew it all and he believed it all, and yet he was restless and unhappy.

One day Cotton Mather resolved to reason it out. He decided to prove to himself beyond any doubt that he was a child of God, forgiven and accepted. So he put down on paper the arguments to prove that he was forgiven. He took the Scriptures and said, 'I believe them, therefore I must believe what they tell me.' He believed in the Lord Jesus Christ as an all-sufficient Saviour – he put that down on paper. And he went through the whole process. And then, he writes, 'I looked in myself for some of the signs and marks of a man who is truly Christian.' What are they? Well, according to 1 Corinthians 11:31–32, confession of sins, self-judging, self-humiliation. He put all that down on paper too, and now he was going to prove to himself that all was well. But this is what he says:

Thus did I try to argue myself into the faith and hope of
my justification, but I must say that I found no spirit in all
this rational way of arguing None of the argument
brought unto my soul the joyful peace which I wanted At
last the Spirit of God powerfully came in upon my heart
and enabled me to receive the pardon of my sin offered
freely unto me with the righteousness of the Lord Jesus
Christ, and this without any distinct considerations on
my having these and those conditions wrought in me.
Then could I, and never till then, rejoice with joy
unspeakable and full of glory afterwards. It was comfortable for me to see in myself the condition of a pardoned
soul.

Here was a man with unusual reasoning ability and
rational powers and he tried to reason himself into an
awareness of God's forgiveness. But he could not. He
was cold. There was no spirit in it. Then suddenly the
Spirit of God did this very thing. There are too many
Christians in the church today whose assurance is
based only upon their deductions. They have been
trained like that. People have said to them, 'Come, look
at this verse – "He that believeth is not condemned."
Do you believe?'

'Yes.'

'Well, you are not condemned, there is your assurance.'

And they stop at that. But that did not satisfy Cotton
Mather, and it should not satisfy any of us. There is a
higher assurance, the assurance given by the blessed
Spirit of God, and it is only he who enables a man or
woman to rejoice with a joy unspeakable and full of
glory, and really to sing with meaning:

Jesus, the very thought of Thee
    With sweetness fills the breast;
But sweeter far Thy face to see,
    And in Thy presence rest.

The love of Jesus, what it is
    None but His loved ones know.
                Bernard of Clairvaux

You either know the love of Jesus or you do not. You cannot really tell anybody what it is; they do not understand. That is this secret element. The master of the feast is astonished, but the servants who draw the water, they know. This secret is only known by those who have received it.

We find the same teaching in Revelation 2:17: 'He that hath an ear, let him hear what the Spirit saith unto the churches; To him that overcometh will I give to eat of the hidden manna, and will give him a white stone, and in the stone a new name written, which no man knoweth saving he that receiveth it.' So here is the question: Are you partaking of the hidden manna – this food, this water, that the world does not know? Our Lord said that about himself when the disciples were worrying because he had not eaten. He said, 'I have meat to eat that ye know not of' (John 4:32). And here it is, the Christian has it, the hidden manna. It is not in the supermarkets. It is not advertised in the papers. The world does not know anything about it, and there are many in the church who know nothing about it. It is 'the *hidden* manna'!

Have you got that white stone with the new name

written on it which no one knows apart from those who have received it? Have you ever prayed to him:

> Write Thy new name upon my heart,
> Thy new best name of love.
>
> *Charles Wesley*

Do you know that he has written it? Have you this secret knowledge of him and his life-giving, satisfying power?

4

A Transforming Blessing

When the ruler of the feast had tasted the water that was made wine, and knew not whence it was: (but the servants which drew the water knew;) the governor of the feast called the bridegroom, and saith unto him, Every man at the beginning doth set forth good wine; and when men have well drunk, then that which is worse: but thou hast kept the good wine until now. This beginning of miracles did Jesus in Cana of Galilee, and manifested forth his glory; and his disciples believed on him.   John 2:9–11

At the end of the twentieth chapter of his Gospel, John says, let me remind you, 'These are written, that ye might believe that Jesus is the Christ, the Son of God; and that believing ye might have life through his name' (John 20:31). This is John's great theme – not only forgiveness, but life. I have suggested that in this Gospel we are given both explicit teaching with regard to that life and also illustrations. The purpose of the miracles is to attest his person, to show who he was, and it is only as we realise who he is that we see that God has put in him this life that we stand in need of, and which is offered to us so freely. So, let me say again, the great questions we should ask ourselves are: Do we possess this life? Can we say honestly with the apostle, 'Of his fulness have all we received, and grace for [upon] grace' (John 1:16)? Can we say with the hymn writer,

> The men of grace have found
>   Glory begun below;
> Celestial fruits on earthly ground
>   From faith and hope may grow.

Can we go on to say honestly:

> The hill of Zion yields
>   A thousand sacred sweets,
> Before we reach the heavenly fields
>   Or walk the golden streets.
>   *Isaac Watts*

Do we know about these 'sacred sweets'? Have we been drinking of the rivers of his grace? Have we partaken of this 'celestial fruit' that by the grace of God is to be obtained and proved even in this world of time? The possibility is held out before us, but is it true of us? I am assuming that we all desire to partake more freely, and in greater fullness, of this 'celestial fruit', this heavenly manna, this 'life which is life indeed', and I am endeavouring to show the way in which that may become an actuality. I have suggested that in this miracle, worked in Cana of Galilee by our Lord, we are given this essential instruction in a very wonderful manner.

We have considered some of the general characteristics but there is still one other to which I must refer before we come to consider the particular blessings which come to us out of this great gift of life. It is that this blessing is always pure and unmixed. This is a very important point. The governor of the feast makes a most interesting statement. He says, 'Every man at the beginning doth set forth good wine; and when men have well drunk, then that which is worse: but thou hast kept the good wine until now.' That is a part of his perplexity. Not only is he amazed at the fact that there is any wine still left, but he is still more amazed at the quality of the wine. This is a complete reversal of everything that he has ever known, of everything that is true of the world.

One of the great, basic characteristics of this life which is in Christ, this fullness of which we can receive, is that it is pure and unmixed, so unlike the world's giving. The world is a fraud. The wise man of the world says: My experience is that on these occasions people have very little of their best wine, but they have any amount of the other, so they serve the best wine at the beginning, and then when people have taken so much of it that their ability to discriminate has gone, the inferior wine is brought out. But the wine our Lord gives is entirely different.

There is nothing more glorious and wonderful about this abundant life than its quality. As the governor of the feast says, it is the way of the world to display the best goods in the shop window. How often have we all had that experience? We pass a shop window and see some wonderful oranges or tomatoes, and go in and buy them. But when we get home and open the bag, the ones we are looking at are very unlike the ones we saw in the window. They put the best in front, then the rest are hidden behind and we are given those. The pretence! The deceit!

The world offers us its so called 'glittering prizes', and the tragedy is that men and women are fooled by it. Sin is always a fraud, it always has this element of deceit. That was the original temptation and the original sin. The devil offered so much, promised so much, but Adam and Eve did not get it. The world gives you something which tastes wonderful at the beginning. It is enticing, attractive, everything seems to be right. But oh, it soon changes. The water fails. There is something putrid and unclean about it. It is not true. It is not honest. It is not 'right through'. It is only a pretence, a sham.

But God offers something entirely different. It is pure – pure through and through, pure from beginning to end. It is described in many ways in the New Testament. The great phrase here in John's Gospel is 'life eternal' (John 17:3). It is life which is life indeed, not a pretence, not an appearance, not something artificial, not something that simulates, but the real thing. It is true.

In his Epistle, John writes, 'God is light, and in him is no darkness at all' (1 John 1:5). It is only of God you can say 'no darkness at all'. He is entirely light, unmixed. And that is the nature of this gift. We are made 'partakers of the divine nature' (2 Peter 1:4). We receive eternal life, the life which is in the Son.

And the glorious thing about the life God gives is that it is not all in the shop window. Of course, sometimes, I am afraid that in their anxiety to get results preachers and evangelists have been guilty of that, but that is a misrepresentation. It is *true*. It is unmixed. It never promises without giving. It is whole. You can call in your analysts, your inspectors, whenever you like, there is no danger here. There is only one quality, so there is no chicanery, no cleverness, no trickery. Here it is in all its purity with the stamp of God himself upon it.

And as the ruler of the feast points out, another thing about God's gift of life is that it is always better even than the world's best. That follows of necessity. What amazes this man is that the good wine comes at the end. The wine that is the result of the miracle is better than anything he had ever known at the beginning. 'This is better than the wine we started with,' he says, and so it is. The Christian life at its very lowest is infinitely superior to everything that the world has to offer us. There will never be a bitter taste. There will never be a sense of disappointment. You will never come across a portion and feel, 'Is this a little bit tainted?' You may examine it minutely, but you will never find anything detracting from it and its glory and its inherent worth.

We cannot afford to pass by any one of these points. And I am sure it is the experience of all who have in any sense ever tasted of this 'heavenly manna', this heavenly gift, that what is taught here is nothing but the simple truth. That is why David is able to say, 'A day in thy courts is better than a thousand' (Psalm 84:10). It is not the amount, it is the quality. David goes on, 'I had rather be a doorkeeper in the house of my God, than to dwell in the tents of wickedness.' It is not the appearance, not the glamour, it is the quality. There is something here that lasts. It never fails. It never disappoints. It is holy. It is God's own gift of everlasting and eternal life, in and through his Son.

Those, then, are the general characteristics of this great gift of life as we find them portrayed here in this illustration which is also a miracle. But now let us move on to the more detailed consideration of it. What is the blessing that comes to us? And it is all here before us in embryo, as it were, in suggestion. The first thing is that it deals with our desperate condition of need. That is obvious in the story. It was terrible to run out of wine at a wedding feast. What a disappointment! What an anti-climax! The wine is finished and they can do nothing.

This is something that we must emphasise about this life that God gives, and this is what makes it so glorious and so wonderful. That is why I have emphasised this element of the miraculous. And that is why there is nothing so romantic in the whole world as a Christian service and preaching the Christian gospel. It is the only thing in the universe that can deal with conditions which are utterly desperate, completely hopeless.

The whole tragedy of the world is that it always fails. It can go so far, but when you are in desperate need, the world can do nothing for you. It just has to abandon you. It cannot deal with its own problems and there-fore it cannot deal with yours. But the whole glory of this abundant life is that it is at this point of utter and complete hopelessness that you begin to see it shining forth in all its glory. It is when you are at the end of everything that you begin to realise what it is.

Now this, again, is one of the laws of the spiritual life. There are many people who know very little about this life – indeed, as we have said, there are many people even in the church who know nothing about it. And the reason for this is that they have never realised their need. They are like the people of Laodicea. They think they have everything and are all right. Believe the gospel? 'Oh yes, always have done.' But they know nothing of the thrill and the glory and the rejoicing. And that is because of this law of the spiritual life, that it is only when we are utterly empty that we begin to receive of the fullness. It is only when we come to the realisation that we can do nothing, nothing at all, that we are completely helpless, and that nobody else can do anything for us, it is only then that we cry out to God and receive his gift of life.

This theme is put before us in many different ways in the Scriptures. We find that in his dealings with his saints God almost invariably leads them into a kind of wilderness. This always precedes the gift we are talking about. And that is, of course, because we must be brought to the point at which we realise our utter dependence on God. And here is this truth in a picture: the wine is finishing. Nobody can do anything. So in her desperation Mary turns to our Lord and more or less commands him to do something.

Now some may feel that by emphasising this I am contradicting what I have been saying previously about the importance of keeping the commandments. 'Whatsoever he saith unto you, do it.' I have said that unless you keep his commandments, unless you are striving

with all your might and main to please him and to do
everything that is well-pleasing in his sight, you might
as well give up any hope of ever knowing this blessing.
Is there not a contradiction here? How can I at one and
the same time say, 'Keep the commandments,' and yet
add that you can do nothing?

Of course, there is no contradiction and for this
reason: the danger lies in *relying* upon keeping the
commandments. Our keeping of the commandments is
merely an expression of our sincerity. If people say, 'I
want this knowledge and yet I want my sin,' then they
are contradicting themselves. They are fools and they
are deluding themselves. So the keeping of the commandments is nothing more than an intense expression
of our desire. That is all. When you want something
from someone, you do everything you can to please
that person. You do not think that by this means you
will purchase that thing, because if you do, and give
that impression, you will get nothing. And it is exactly
the same here. The keeping of the commandments is a
proof that I really am more concerned about this than
anything else, and that there is nothing that I would not
do to be well-pleasing in his sight.

But I also realise that if I have done everything, it is
still nothing. Our Lord makes this clear in his statement to the disciples when they were expecting some
kind of reward. He says in effect, 'You have not got
this right at all.' He says this after giving a parable of a
man who sent his servants out to the field to work.
They worked hard all day, and returned in the evening
feeling very tired, but he still expected them to wait on
him at the table. Our Lord says, 'When ye shall have

done all those things which are commanded you, say, We are unprofitable servants: we have done that which was our duty to do' (Luke 17:10).

The moment we rely upon our activity, the activity is useless. Our obedience is nothing more than an intense expression of the fact that there is nothing that I would not do, though I know that all I do is nothing, and all my righteousness is but as filthy rags. It is he who gives. It is he alone who can give. 'Thou must save, and Thou alone' wrote A. M. Toplady. We must realise that we are utterly bankrupt and there is nothing left. That is the prelude, the invariable prelude.

I could illustrate this at great length from the lives of the saints. They all seem to reach a point of exhaustion, and even physical suffering. You find this in Whitefield's journals. He went through a phase in which he was desperately ill and it was only then, in that condition of complete failure and of final exhaustion, when he felt that the end had come, that suddenly he was visited in a great and glorious way by the Holy Spirit, and the promises of God were sealed to him.

And the same thing exactly was true of the two brothers John and Charles Wesley. Read their journals. Read their account of how they both came to the end of their tether and saw the uselessness of all the good works on which they had formerly relied. They had done many good works. They had given up great positions. They had crossed the Atlantic to preach to pagans in Georgia – there was nothing, in a sense, that they had not done. But they saw that it was all useless, dung and refuse. They were longing for this knowledge and this life. But they could not find it, and they both reached the point of exhaustion and became physically ill. No wine – nothing to be done. They could not do anything, nor could anybody else. And then suddenly, unexpectedly, when they least anticipated it, he came.

As long as we are self-reliant we will never know this fullness. You can be a Christian – let us be clear about this, I am not saying you are not a Christian – you can be a Christian without knowing this fullness. But I am showing the difference between existing in the Christian life and enjoying the life fully. I am drawing the distinction between the bread and butter of the Christian life and enjoying the banquet. We are dealing with the banquet. 'Of his fulness have all we received.' That is what we are meant to receive. That is what is offered to us. 'That ye might be filled,' as Paul puts it to the Ephesians, 'with all the fulness of God' (Ephesians 3:19). The people who have arrived in God's banqueting chamber are always those who have known what it is to be in rags and tatters, shivering and exhausted out in the street with nothing to eat. But suddenly the door opens and a hand appears and they are drawn in.

Then a second characteristic of the blessing is that it entirely changes the whole position. Water into wine! Need into profusion! This is Christianity: it is transforming. The idea that Christianity is something you add on to your life, a decision to live a better life or to go in for this or that – oh, how remote it is from everything that we are looking at here! It is a transforming action of the power of God. Nothing less. 'Born of the Spirit.' 'Born again.' 'Born from above.' An infusion of the divine nature in each person: *The Life of God in the Soul of Man*. It is barrenness transformed into sufficiency, concern and apprehension into rejoicing.

Eight hundred years before the coming of our Lord, Isaiah saw and described it all. That is why he is called 'the evangelical prophet'. What is the difference that Christ makes? Here it is: 'Beauty for ashes, the oil of joy for mourning, the garment of praise for the spirit of heaviness' (Isaiah 61:3). From the ashes and the dung-hill and the rags and the tatters to beauty. This is the nature of the transformation.

The people are mourning, seeking and searching. 'Oh that I knew where I might find him,' sighs Job (Job 23:3).

> O Love Divine, how sweet Thou art!
>   When shall I find my willing heart
> All taken up with Thee?
> I thirst, I faint, I die to prove
> The greatness of redeeming love,
>   The love of God to me.
>   *Charles Wesley*

But I cannot. Have you known this longing? My point is that until you know it, you will never know the answer and the fullness. But once you have known this longing and say, 'I thirst, I faint, I die,' then you can expect God's transforming life to come suddenly to you. Then you will have 'the oil of joy' for that 'mourning', which goes in a moment. You will have 'the garment of praise for the spirit of heaviness'.

Oh the spirit of heaviness! Do you know anything about it? The Bible is full of this. The apostle Paul writing to the Romans says, 'For ye have not received the spirit of bondage again to fear' (Romans 8:15). But so many of us are in a spirit of bondage and fear. There is no joy, no abandon. 'No,' Paul says, 'ye have the Spirit of adoption, whereby we cry, Abba, Father.' That is what we are talking about.

Isaiah puts this in a very interesting way. He writes, 'And the parched ground shall become a pool' (Isaiah 35:7). I prefer the other translation which suggests that 'parched ground' be translated by 'the mirage': 'The mirage shall [actually] become a pool.' Have you been walking that road? Have you been travelling through that desert? There you are, exhausted and weak and thirsty, and you see a pool and you are beginning to rejoice. But when you arrive, it is nothing – it is a mirage. That is the experience even of the saints of God who have known this great fullness. They have been deluded by many a mirage. But at last 'the mirage becomes a pool' and they begin to drink of it and bathe in it, and are filled with this extraordinary fullness.

Or take it as Ezekiel puts it. God says, 'I will take the stony heart out of their flesh, and will give them an heart of flesh' (Ezekiel 11:19). What a contrast! A stony heart, hard, unfeeling, allowing a little bit of dutiful sentiment, perhaps, but with no depth of feeling, no fundamental emotion. But, 'I will take out of you the stony heart, and I will give you a heart of flesh.'

The New Testament way of putting this is even more striking: 'You hath he quickened,' says Paul, 'who were dead in trespasses and sins' (Ephesians 2:1). There is no greater contrast than the contrast between death and life. From being dead you find yourself alive and thrilling with a new vitality.

Or look at it as it is exemplified in the history of the early church. There is the apostle Peter preaching on the Day of Pentecost, preaching a very convicting sermon. And as he preaches we are told that the people listening are 'pricked in their heart', and they cry out in an anguish saying, 'Men and brethren, what shall we do?' (Acts 2:37). An agony, a crisis, a desperation, an utter hopelessness. Then as we continue reading we find that later they are eating 'with gladness and singleness of heart' in one another's houses, rejoicing together in God (Acts 2:46). What a transformation! Water to wine! Look at the Philippian jailor, pulling out his sword on the point of committing suicide, and asking his question, 'Sirs, what must I do to be saved?' (Acts 16:30). The anguish again, the desperation, but then, in a moment, he 'rejoiced, believing in God with all his house' (verse 34).

The Ethiopian eunuch shows exactly the same transformation – perplexity, unhappiness as he tries to understand, but cannot, followed by 'rejoicing' after his meeting with Philip (Acts 8:39).

Now this, I say again, is the great characteristic of this blessing. There is nothing partial about it. It really changes the entire situation. Mr Spurgeon put it like this: 'The difference between the Christian who knows what it is to have received of this fullness, and the Christian who does not know that, is greater than the difference between that second Christian and the man who is not a Christian at all.' That is a tremendous statement, but I believe it is true. There is, of course, a striking difference between the non-Christian and the Christian, but it is not as great as the difference between the man who has been saved, the man who believes in Christ and believes he is forgiven but has very little more than that, and the man who is receiving the heavenly manna. 'The men of faith have found glory begun below' – some knowledge of the glory, some foretaste of it, some insight into it. Nothing else comes in any sense anywhere near this. To have a glimpse of that glory is in itself greater than the whole universe. Do we know it? Do we belong to the 'men of grace'? Have you found 'glory begun below'?

The next thing I would emphasise about this fullness is that you know when this has happened to you, you know when you have received it. In other words, we must emphasise the whole aspect of assurance and certainty. This is an important point because there is a popular teaching which emphasises the formula: 'Take it by faith.' This is important because that teaching is concerned about the very thing we are dealing with. It says to each believer, 'Now you are a Christian, there is no doubt about that. But you are not enjoying the Christian life as you should. You are defeated and depressed. Do you want this fullness? And if you do, this is the answer: It is all there for you in Christ. Take it by faith. Believe in it.'

But then someone replies, 'Well, I've done that but I don't feel any different.'

So this teaching says, 'But you must not consider your feelings. Do not worry about them. Take it by faith. It's offered to you in the Bible. You've believed the Scripture, so all you must do is say, "I want this, I believe it is there." And you must not stop there. You must say, "I believe that as I now ask for it, I have

received it," and you then thank God for it.' Because
you have taken it by faith, you have received it.

That is the instruction given, but you feel exactly as
you did before. You are not conscious of any difference.

Now that, it seems to me, is a complete reversal of
what we are taught here in John's Gospel because,
surely, on the very surface it is apparent that this blessing is something that not only happens, but makes us
aware of the fact that it has happened. It is impossible
for it to happen to you without your knowing it. You
can be a Christian, I say again, without having assurance of salvation, but you cannot partake of his fullness, in a real sense, without knowing that you have
done so.

In other words, this doctrine of assurance and of certainty is vital to the whole teaching about fullness.
Again, let me quote to you Romans 8:15–17, 'For ye
have not received the spirit of bondage again to fear;
but ye have received the Spirit of adoption, whereby
we cry, Abba, Father. The Spirit itself also beareth witness with our spirit, that we are the children of God:
And if children, then heirs; heirs of God, and joint-
heirs with Christ.' Now that is it. We know! 'For I
know whom I have believed' (2 Timothy 1:12). I am
persuaded. I am certain. That is the language of the
apostle Paul. Indeed, it is the language of all the New
Testament writers. Take, for example, that crucial
statement in 1 Peter 1:8, 'Whom having not seen, ye
love; in whom, though now ye see him not, yet believing, ye rejoice with joy unspeakable and full of glory.'

You see, this teaching, as we find it elaborated in the

fourteenth chapter of John's Gospel, is a teaching which tells us that God and the Lord Jesus Christ come into us and take up their abode within us. Or see how Paul puts it in the Epistle to the Ephesians. Paul is writing to believers; he is assured that his readers are true believers, but he says, 'I bow my knees unto the Father of our Lord Jesus Christ' – he is praying unceasingly for them, and he is praying 'that he would grant you, according to the riches of his glory, to be strengthened with might by his Spirit in the inner man; that Christ may dwell in your hearts by faith' (Ephesians 3:14, 16–17).

Now that is it. You can be in Christ, you can be a believer, you can know that your sins are forgiven, yes, but the vital question is: Do you know that Christ is dwelling in your heart?

In the book of Revelation, the letter to the Laodicean church says, 'Behold, I stand at the door, and knock.' That is not a message to unbelievers but to believers. 'I stand at the door, and knock: if any man hear my voice, and open the door, I will come in to him, and will sup with him' (Revelation 3:20). That is what I am talking about, and I am saying that when he comes in and sups, you know he is there. You do not 'take this by faith'. You do not remain exactly as you were before. Your feelings are not undisturbed or unmoved or unstimulated. No, no, the Guest has come in: you *know*!

If you read the accounts of any one of the great revivals in the history of the church, you will often come across this point. Recently I was reading again about the great Evangelical Awakening of the eighteenth century and I cannot remember how many times I read of people who, during a time of unusual blessing, became aware of their bankruptcy. They knew they were Christians, but they said, 'I do not *know* him. I do not know him personally. I do not know what it is to have my heart ravished by his visitations. I really do not know what it is to commune with him and to sup with him. I believe in him, but I cannot say that I know him in this sense.' They were convicted and longed to know Christ dwelling in the heart by faith. Many passed through agonies – hungering, thirsting, crying, fainting. And then the record tells us that one would suddenly shout, 'He is come! He is come!' And from the mourning and the agonising a smile would appear on their faces. They would begin to praise him and to thank him. They might even shout. They might even sing. There were some who would dance! The glory! 'He is come!' The blessed Guest had entered in and they knew it. Of course they knew it! Is it conceivable that this could happen to anybody without their knowing it?

No, you do not 'take it by faith'. You believe in the possibility – that is where faith comes in. You believe that this is not some scriptural hyperbole, but that it is really true in experience, that it happened at the beginning, that it has happened throughout the centuries and that it can happen to you. But you do not thank him for having come and still say, 'I do not know whether he has come or not.' I know of nothing that is more dangerous than this teaching which tells us to take it by faith. I know many people who have claimed to have taken so much by faith, but they have seemed to me to be bankrupt.

And, of course, to take an analogy which I think settles it, they use exactly the same teaching with regard to faith healing.

'Have you not heard this?' they say. 'Now then, do you believe that Christ can heal?'

You say, 'Yes.'

'Very well,' they say, 'ask him to heal you.'

So the sick person says, 'All right,' and asks him to heal.

Then the instructor says, 'Do you really believe that?'

'I do.'

'Well very well, then, you believe that he can do it, you believe that he is ready to answer all those who ask him?'

'I do.'

'You have asked him. Very well. Now then thank him. Thank him for having healed you.' And the sick person is made to do that.

I have known many very unhappy souls who did thank God in faith in that way but discovered that they had never been healed at all. And sometimes this has resulted in tragedy. In the biography of Andrew Murray we read that his nephew, who was suffering from advanced tuberculosis, wanted to go with him on a preaching tour. Andrew Murray at this point believed in faith healing in the sense I have just described, and he and his nephew thanked God for the healing. But the poor nephew was dead in three weeks' time!

When you are healed, you know it. And that is true of the fullness. You ask in faith. You agonise in faith. You long in faith. But when it is given you, when it happens, you are not uncertain. You say, 'He is come! He is come!' You know that you have received of his fullness, and grace for grace.

But not only do you know when it has happened, everybody else knows. 'When the ruler of the feast had tasted the water that was made wine, and knew not whence it was (but the servants which drew the water knew;) the governor of the feast called the bridegroom, and saith unto him, Every man at the beginning doth set forth good wine; and when men have well drunk, then that which is worse: but thou hast kept the good wine until now.' He knows! And so do the servants, and the guests.

Is not this the thing that strikes us as we read in the Book of Acts of the coming of the Holy Spirit upon the hundred and twenty believers in the upper room? They knew. They were filled with rejoicing and exultation, and 'began to speak in other tongues'. They knew, and everybody else, the whole of Jerusalem, knew. This cannot be hidden.

Look at Peter in the house of Cornelius. When some of the Christians in Jerusalem were criticising Peter for admitting the Gentiles into the Christian church, he replied by reciting this story. He said in effect, 'There I was preaching, and as I was preaching the Holy Spirit fell on them as it did on us at the beginning. Who was I therefore to withhold baptism from them?' (Acts 11:1–18). God had given the evidence and Peter could see it. Not only did they know, he knew.

This is confirmed in the long story and history of the Christian church. That is what is really meant by revival. People outside the church look at Christian men

and women whom they have known all their lives, and
see them going to their chapels and churches, and
rather despise them. They say, 'They are traditionalists,
just going to church for the sake of going, but I have to
live with them, I have to work with them, and I know
that their Christianity makes no difference to them at
all.' Then suddenly a revival comes and the workmate
sees that something has happened. That friend has
something real now, something true, something vital.
That is why such times of revival in the church are
always great evangelistic times. The world is convinced
by what it sees. It has ocular demonstration, as it were.
It sees the transformation. Not only do Christians
themselves know it, not only are they feasting on the
heavenly manna and enjoying this heavenly fruit, but
everybody who knows them can see that something
vital, something transforming, has happened to them.
Their neighbours and workmates are now ready to
listen to their testimony to the Lord Jesus Christ.

So let us ask ourselves the question: Can I say
honestly, 'He is come'? Do I know him? Have I had
any personal dealings with him? Have I begun to sup
with him? Have I tasted of this heavenly manna, this
'life which is life indeed'?

5

A Superabundance of Blessing

When the ruler of the feast had tasted the water that was made wine, and knew not whence it was: (but the servants which drew the water knew;) the governor of the feast called the bridegroom, and saith unto him, Every man at the beginning doth set forth good wine; and when men have well drunk, then that which is worse: but thou hast kept the good wine until now. This beginning of miracles did Jesus in Cana of Galilee, and manifested forth his glory; and his disciples believed on him.   John 2:9–11

We are studying John's account of the wedding at Cana not only because it is a record of a historical event but because it is a miracle. The Son of God here on earth worked miracles – it was one of his ways, as John puts it, of showing us, of giving a sign, that he is indeed the Son of God. But we are interested in this incident primarily because it is at the same time a parable. John's theme in his Gospel is that our Lord came to give us life which is life indeed, and this incident shows us how this fullness, this 'grace upon grace', is to be received.

We have seen negative instructions – what we are not to do – and we have looked at what we must do. Now we are examining the character, or the nature, of the blessing. We have shown that it is a blessing that always comes in response to a condition of desperation and that when our Lord acts he changes the entire situation. That is what he does here: from need he provides satisfaction. And that is what he always does. And then we went on to show how that when our Lord acts, it is always clear and evident.

But now I want to show you something of the fullness of the satisfaction that our Lord gives. This comes out so clearly here. He does not merely turn just a little water into wine, there is a sufficiency, a superabundance. We find many illustrations of that. It is so typical of our Lord that when he fed the five thousand with five barley loaves and two fish, at the end of the meal, the disciples collected twelve basketfuls of broken pieces that were left over and above what was needed (Matthew 14:15–21). That is his method; it is always this overflowing sufficiency. This is emphasised right through the New Testament and that is why it is so important for us. If we receive of his fullness, then there is this element of superabundance.

We see adumbrations and foreshadowings of this in the Old Testament. By the eye of faith the psalmist is able to see something of it, and he puts it like this: 'My cup runneth over' (Psalm 23:5). It is not merely just full, it is 'running over', filled to the brim and overflowing. That is the characteristic of God's grace – not only its freedom but its fullness, its abundance, its all-sufficiency.

The Song of Solomon is undoubtedly a picture and a prophecy of the relationship between Christ and his church. Written in a poetic, dramatic form, it is a perfect representation of the church as the bride of Christ. This is a New Testament term but the Song of Solomon sees it long before it came to pass. This is how Solomon describes God's overflowing love: 'He brought me to the banqueting house . . .' – and that is where he always brings us. It is not to some kind of 'soup kitchen', or to some temporary place where we can be given just a little food to keep us from starvation. No, no! It is a 'banqueting house'! '. . . and his banner over me was love. Stay me with flagons, comfort me with apples: for I am sick of [sick with, faint with] love' (Song of Solomon 2:4–5). There is so much love that it is almost overwhelming me.

This is brought out equally in verses 11–13 of the same chapter: 'For, lo, the winter is past, the rain is over and gone.' That is the test that we apply to ourselves: Are we living in a kind of spiritual winter? We are not meant to be like that. What is the condition of our soul? Is it like a day which is overcast, cloudy, drizzling, foggy, 'neither hot nor cold' (Revelation 3:15)? No! When he visits the heart, when he exerts the glory of his power, when he grants us the fullness of his Spirit, he says to us, 'The winter is past, the rain is over and gone; the flowers appear on the earth; the time of the singing of birds is come, and the voice of the turtle is heard in our land; the fig tree putteth forth her green figs, and the vines with the tender grape give a good smell. Arise, my love, my fair one, and come away.'

In other places in the Old Testament we find the same suggestion of overflowing abundance. Isaiah writes: 'The wilderness' – the desolate place – 'shall be glad ... The parched ground shall become a pool' (Isaiah 35:1, 7). 'Then shall the lame man leap as an hart' (Isaiah 35:6). That is the language and imagery of the Old Testament, as it puts this teaching so plainly to us. It can all be summed up in the sixteenth verse of that second chapter of the Song of Solomon. The effect of this love is to make us say, 'My beloved is mine, and I am his.'

But when we come to the New Testament, of course, the richness of God's blessing, seen in a pictorial form in Cana of Galilee, is made much more explicit. Our Lord says it clearly many times. There is no more beautiful illustration than his conversation with the woman of Samaria. There she is at a well where she has come to draw water. One of the hard tasks of her life is having to go to the well to draw water. In the middle of the day – when Jesus speaks to her – the heat is terrible, and drawing water is an awful burden. So there she is at the well, and our Lord asks her for a drink of water. Then he says, 'If thou knewest the gift of God, and who it is that saith to thee, Give me to drink; thou wouldest have asked of him, and he would have given thee living water' (John 4:10). The woman does not understand this, so our Lord expounds it to her. He says, 'Whosoever drinketh of this water shall thirst again' (verse 13). Now that is life in this world, is it not? Permanent satisfaction? Never! There will be a thirst and a need to come again. You have to keep on going back to the well to get a little more water, just to keep you going.

The tragedy is that many of us are living that sort of desperate Christian life. Sunday comes and we get some strength, and then we lose some on Monday; a good deal is gone by Tuesday and we wonder whether we have anything left. On Wednesday it has all gone and then we exist. Or perhaps refreshment comes in some other way, some meeting we attend, some friends we meet. . . .

Now that is the old order of things, that is not the new. So our Lord goes on to put it like this: 'Whosoever drinketh of this water shall thirst again: but whosoever drinketh of the water that I shall give him shall never thirst; but the water that I shall give him shall be in him a well of water springing up into everlasting life' (verses 13–14). He puts a well *within* us. We are not always drawing from somewhere outside. The well, the spring, goes on springing up from within into everlasting life.

Or listen to him again – I am just trying to show you that this is the great theme of this Gospel in particular, though it is the theme of the whole of the New Testament. This is true Christianity. 'In the last day, that great day of the feast, Jesus stood and cried, saying, If any man thirst, let him come unto me, and drink. He that believeth on me, as the scripture hath said, out of his belly [out of his innermost parts] shall flow rivers of living water' (John 7:37–38). Rivers! From inside, from the depth of one's being, there shall flow out – oh, not just a little trickle but 'rivers of living water'. And John explains it. 'This spake he of the Spirit, which they that believe on him should receive: for the Holy Ghost was not yet given; because that Jesus was not yet glorified' (verse 39).

And when we come on to the Book of Acts, we read that the Spirit was poured out on the Day of Pentecost. That is the term that is used – 'poured out'. Nothing is ever said about this except we get this impression of profusion. It is overwhelming; it is a baptism; it is a shower coming upon us and it is unmistakable. So we are told that on the Day of Pentecost the believers were all 'filled with the Holy Ghost' (Acts 2:4). Filled! And we find the same term in Acts 4:31, and in many other places.

And then take the way the apostle Paul puts it in Romans 5:5: 'The love of God,' he says, 'is shed abroad in our hearts.' It is not just a little touch of moisture but love is poured out, 'shed abroad' in a great profusion – 'shed abroad in our hearts by the Holy Ghost which is given unto us'. And all the other terms have the same meaning. 'The fruit of the Spirit,' says Paul, and we think at once of an orchard where the trees are groaning with fruit. 'The fruit of the Spirit is love, joy, peace, longsuffering, gentleness, goodness, faith, meekness, temperance' (Galatians 5:22–23). There is great profusion.

And then, of course, the apostle surpasses himself at the end of Ephesians 3. He has already talked about 'the unsearchable riches of Christ' (3:8); he has mentioned 'the exceeding riches of his grace' (2:7). He brings out all his superlatives and still it is not enough. So he can say nothing beyond this: 'that ye might be filled with all the fulness of God' (Ephesians 3:19).

God is eternal. There is no limit to him. All his qualities are absolutes, and his fullness is endless; it is eternal.

Then, writing in a very personal and tender manner to the Philippians, though he was in prison, the apostle uses terms which are quite extraordinary when we think of his position. He is in prison. He is suffering in body. He says he has become an old man before his time. Elsewhere he calls himself 'Paul, the aged' (Philemon 9). He is on the verge of death, and it is going to be a very cruel death. Yet he says, 'I have all, and abound: I am full' (Philippians 4:18). Now what more can a man say than that? There is a man who has received of his fullness, and grace upon grace.

John says the same thing: we have life, he says, and this life is in us. There is a seed that remains in us (1 John 3:9). And Peter says we are 'partakers of the divine nature' (2 Peter 1:4). There is nothing beyond this, and the New Testament writers all vye with one another to try to give some impression of this fullness and superabundance of life that they have received through the Spirit in Christ Jesus.

That, then, is what the Bible says – in the Old Testament, giving the preview and in the New Testament, showing the fullness. 'But,' says somebody, 'that's all right; but surely that was only for New Testament times. We must not take New Testament history too literally. That was the beginning of the church, and things like that only happened at the beginning. You don't expect it to continue in that way.'

Well, I would have thought that that view is a great denial of Scripture. The moment you begin to speak like that you are denying the teaching of the New

Testament. 'The promise,' says the New Testament, 'is unto you, and to your children, and to all that are afar off' (Acts 2:39). If I believed that what I am told here in the New Testament was only for the first generation of Christians and not for us today, I would not be in this pulpit.

The statement made by those people is a lie. And, of course, it is not only wrong as an understanding of the Scriptures, it is falsified completely by the long history of the Christian church.

This is why one sometimes thinks that the best thing for people to do is to read the history of the church and the lives of the saints. There, in almost every century, we see the continuation of what is described here. In the early centuries we read the thrilling account of the first Christians, the confessors and the martyrs – what a glorious body of people they were! We read of how they rejoiced in their sufferings for Christ. The spectators sitting in their comfortable seats in the arena in Rome and looking at 'these unfortunate people, these nobodies' being thrown to the lions, were staggered by the heavenly brightness which they could see shining from the faces of these Christians. It was this 'life', this 'fullness', Christ in them, making them 'more than conquerors' (Romans 8:37) as the New Testament had prophesied they would be.

Then as we move on through the centuries we find exactly the same thing. In all ages, in all countries, continents, climes, it is always the same. Perhaps we see more personal records of this in the eighteenth century than at any other time, although in the seventeenth century we read the amazing testimonies of many of the

Puritans. But when we come to the eighteenth century, we read of people like Jonathan Edwards and his wife, and Whitefield, and Howel Harries, and the Wesley brothers, and see how they were overwhelmed by the joy of God's fullness.

Whitefield preached so much – even too much – that he was physically exhausted and could scarcely stand. His friends persuaded him to lie down on his bed and have a rest, but he could not rest. Why? Because Christ was manifesting his love in such profusion and superabundance that he was thrilled by it and sleep was impossible. That is the kind of thing about which we are speaking. That is what is shown us here in this parable, in this miracle that was wrought at Cana in Galilee.

I could go on for a very long time quoting such experiences out of the diaries and journals of these various men, but God forbid that anybody again should say, 'But there you are dealing with very outstanding men.' Well, I agree I am dealing with outstanding and unusually gifted men, but they were human beings like all of us, and there was a time in their lives when, for all their brilliant gifts, they were very unhappy people – as we have already seen.

You do not explain what happened to them in terms of personality or in terms of human abilities or propensities or powers; they were the same before and after. No, this was the gift of God. As I am showing you, this was the action of the Lord Jesus Christ. The situation remained hopeless until he decided to act, then the whole position was entirely changed.

And what is so wonderful, therefore, is that we find

this experience of God not only in the lives of outstanding men, great preachers, great thinkers and
others, but also in the lives of the most ordinary
people. And that is why we should thank God that
these greater men have recorded some of the experiences told them by these others whose names are not
even remembered. But they participated in the same
thing. At every time of revival there is no distinction
between great and small. The 'wind bloweth where it
listeth' (John 3:8), and the Spirit chooses people of all
types. You will find some of the most ordinary people
filled until their hearts are overflowing and almost
incapable of expressing what has happened to them.

Now that is what we must realise: it is his action, and
when he acts, he 'sheds abroad', he 'pours forth', with
the result that out of our innermost parts flow 'streams
of living water', and it is overwhelming.

John Ryland sums this up so well:

> No good in creatures can be found
> But may be found in Thee;
> I must have all things and abound,
> While God is God to me.
> He that has made my heaven secure
> Will here all good provide.

Then:

> While Christ is rich, can I be poor?
> What can I want beside?
> *John Ryland*

I am in Christ; he is the Head of the body. There is

an intimate organic relationship. So John Ryland puts the logical question, 'While Christ is rich' – he is the Lord of glory, the Lord of everything – 'While Christ is rich, can I be poor?' Beloved Christian people, there is something wrong somewhere, is there not? We are in him, we belong to him, he is our Head, we are his people and he is so rich – 'the unsearchable riches of Christ' – so how can we be poor? What is the matter? Why do we not receive of his fullness?

It is all due to our failure to realise the riches that are in him and our relationship to him. We listen to the devil, we listen to our adversary, we listen to our own vain thoughts, instead of believing the Scriptures. And here, in the glory of the wedding of Cana, God, in his infinite tenderness through the Spirit, has even put it for us in a pictorial form. We are like the people in the feast who say, 'There is no more wine.' And we look to him, and he rises, and he gives the command, and there is a superabundance.

Listen to Anna Laetitia Waring:

> In heavenly love abiding,
>   No change my heart shall fear;
> And safe is such confiding,
>   For nothing changes here:
>
> Wherever He may guide me,
>   No want shall turn me back;
> My Shepherd is beside me,
>   And nothing can I lack:
> His wisdom ever waketh,
>   His sight is never dim;
> He knows the way He taketh,
>   And I will walk with Him

We sing these glorious hymns but these people did not write them primarily because they were poets. There are many poets who do not write things like this, quite the opposite. Many poets, like Keats, were atheists or agnostics. They could not write hymns like this, because they knew nothing about it. But hymn-writers record their experience. Take Charles Wesley. He was a poet in his own right, and even if he had never been a Christian he would have been an outstanding poet. He says,

> Thou, O Christ, art all I want;
> More than all in Thee I find

And then he goes on:

> Plenteous grace with Thee is found,
>   Grace to cover all my sin;
> Let the healing streams abound,
>   Make me, keep me pure within.
> Thou of life the fountain art.

That is it! 'In him was life, and the life was the light of men' (John 1:4).

> Thou of life the fountain art,
> Freely let me take of Thee;
> Spring Thou up within my heart,
> Rise to all eternity.
>   *Charles Wesley*

That is glorious poetry, is it not? But it is true experience. There was a time when Charles Wesley could not have written those words, but from May 1738 he was able to write like that.

Then listen to another writer:

> Loved with everlasting love,
>   Led by grace that love to know;
> Spirit, breathing from above,
>   Thou hast taught me it is so.
> O this full this perfect peace!
>   O this transport all divine!
> In a love which cannot cease,
>   I am His, and He is mine.
>   *George Wade Robinson*

Do you hear the echo of the Song of Solomon? It is the experience of God's people throughout the centuries, in spite of all variations in circumstances and conditions.

So can we appropriate this language in any measure? This is what is being offered us in the New Testament. This is true Christianity. Not men and women struggling to hold on, and, with a great effort of the will, just managing to keep themselves religious. That is a terrible contradiction of what we have here!

And, of course, that is what has antagonised so many non-Christians. If we give the impression that the main effect of Christianity is to make us miserable, then it is not surprising that ninety per cent of the people are outside the Christian church. 'Miserable Christians,' they say, 'look at them!' And they add that *they* have life, *they* have joy, *they* have fullness. Shame on us Christian people!

But it is not merely a question of saying shame on us.

What a terrible responsibility is ours if we are so mis-representing this 'glorious gospel of the blessed God' (1 Timothy 1:11). We are meant to be witnesses to all people that we are filled to overflowing. We are meant to show the truth of the psalmist's words: 'My cup runneth over!' (Psalm 23:5).

My next point is that this is not one isolated experience in someone's life. Now many fall into the trap of thinking this. No, it goes on and increases. The wine that Jesus provides at Cana is not just a temporary supply to the marriage guests which quickly runs out. No, no; it is enough for the whole occasion until the wedding is over.

And that is a picture of what he does in our lives. Indeed, there is a phrase here which puts it very beautifully and will help us to remember it. The governor of the feast says, 'Every man at the beginning doth set forth good wine; and when men have well drunk, then that which is worse: *but thou hast kept the good wine until now.*' Not the beginning but *now*, much later on, when the proceedings have gone on for some time and it is towards the end. And this is something very wonderful: the best is at the end.

Now many fail at this point. I have always found it depressing to listen to the kind of people who, whenever you meet them, will always for sure tell you the story of their conversion many years ago. They tell you that story every time. I have known people do exactly the same thing with revival. Now there is a sense in which I can understand this. There is always something about an initial experience that is remarkable and outstanding. And a time of revival is so amazing and wonderful that it is not surprising that people go on talking about it. But, if they give the impression that they have had nothing since that wonderful experience, that ever after they have been walking through a wilderness, and travelling through a desert, then it is absolutely wrong. But there are many Christian people like that. Their idea of the Christian life is of a dramatic experience, perhaps at the outset, after which they just trudge along, living on the strength of that and partly keeping their eye turned backwards as they go forward. But this is quite wrong. It is almost a denial of this essential principle that I am outlining – and thank God that it is! What a tragedy it would be if it were only the beginning of the Christian life which could be described in this way!

I remember once – forgive me for giving a personal story, I do it in order to illustrate my point – I remember I was preaching in a certain part of the country and staying with a man who was the Chairman of the Education Committee of his county. We were invited by the headmaster of the local grammar school to address the children in the afternoon. On the platform, I made this older man speak first, before me. He was a jovial type of man, and he did what I anticipated he would do. He looked at the children and said, 'Boys and girls, what wouldn't I give if I could only be back where you are! That was a wonderful time! Oh to be a boy again! I am an old man now, and if I could only go back, I would give the whole world!'

Well, when my time came, I said the exact opposite. I said, 'Boys and girls, I thank God I am not sitting where you are! I thank God, because I can tell you life gets better as it goes on.'

And it can. I meant it. I still mean it. But there is a negative attitude that comes even into the Christian life, and it is wrong, it is a denial. The Old Testament is clear about this. Here is the psalmist, writing under the old dispensation, and this is how he puts it: 'The righteous shall flourish like the palm tree: he shall grow like a cedar in Lebanon. Those that be planted in the house of the Lord shall flourish in the courts of our God. They shall still bring forth fruit in old age; they shall be fat and flourishing' (Psalm 92:12–14). (Did you know before where the expression 'fat and flourishing' came from?)

Thank God that Psalm 92 is true. If I am not a better preacher now than I was thirty years ago, shame upon me! This is a growing life; it is an increasing life. We do not just live on some original resources. No, no! The Christian life is not merely one experience. It goes on being repeated. And, 'The best is yet to be!' The best is at the end. Listen to God's words to the prophet Isaiah: 'And even to your old age I am he; and even to hoar hairs will I carry you: I have made, and I will bear; even I will carry, and I will deliver you' (Isaiah 46:4). God does not merely start and then abandon us. No, no. He has said, 'I will never leave thee, nor forsake thee' (Hebrews 13:5).

But come to the New Testament statement of all this and see how Paul, rising to one of his great mountain-tops at the end of the third chapter of 2 Corinthians, says, 'We all, with open face beholding' – and it means 'going on beholding' – 'as in a glass the glory of the

Lord, are changed into the same image from glory to glory' (2 Corinthians 3:18). That is it. That is the Christian life. It is progressive. It expands and increases as we are 'changed from glory into glory'. We do not just get born again and then remain there, static, holding on to what we have, rather giving the impression that we have lost something wonderful and that the great thrill we had at the beginning has gone. That is machinery, not life. This is a life that changes us 'from glory into glory', and it is endless and eternal.

Again, let the poets express it for us:

> Streams of mercy never ceasing
> Call for songs of loudest praise.
> *Robert Robinson*

That is the characteristic of this life. The hymn, 'In heavenly love abiding', which I quoted earlier, goes on to say this:

> Green pastures are before me,
>   Which yet I have not seen;
> Bright skies will soon be o'er me,
>   Where the dark clouds have been:
> My hope I cannot measure,
>   My path to life is free;
> My Saviour has my treasure,
>   And He will walk with me.
> *Anna Laetitia Waring*

'For now we see through a glass, darkly; but then face to face: now I know in part; but then shall I know even as also I am known' (1 Corinthians 13:12).

Again, if you examine the lives of the saints, I think you will see that this is constantly found in all their records, and, I say again, thank God for this! They went on enjoying this life, and it went on deepening and increasing. Then when we come to look at them on their deathbeds, we find, as John Wesley put it, 'Our people die well.' Indeed, some of them had their greatest experiences of all on their deathbed. There they received in yet greater measure than they had received before.

The effect, then, is that our faith is increased. That is why John leaves the account of the miracle at Cana of Galilee with these words: 'This beginning of miracles did Jesus in Cana of Galilee, and manifested forth his glory; and his disciples believed on him.' Now they had already believed in him. That is the point – they were already disciples and they had already believed – but as the result of this they believed more than ever. And that is one of the great principles and rules in the whole of the Christian life – the more you receive, the more you desire. It encourages you, it gives you proof, and you know, and therefore you seek him more and more.

That is Paul's argument in Philippians. Here is a man who had experienced so much but he still tells us that his desire is, 'That I may know him' – Paul knows him, that is why he desires to know him, he wants more and more – 'and the power of his resurrection, and the fellowship of his sufferings' (3:10). And Paul continues in verse 12, 'Not as though I had already attained . . .' By that he means: I have not got it all. I have not arrived at the end. I have not exhausted it. 'Not as though I had already attained, either were already perfect: but I follow after, if that I may apprehend that for which also I am apprehended of Christ Jesus. Brethren, I count not myself to have apprehended' – I have not got there – 'but this one thing I do, forgetting those things which are behind' – and I sometimes feel like telling many Christian people that: Forget what has happened to you. What is happening to you now is the question. And what are you expecting? 'Forgetting the things which are behind, and reaching forth unto those things which are before. I press toward the mark for the prize of the high calling of God in Christ Jesus' (verses 12–14).

The effect of all this, then, should be to make us utter something like this:

> O Lord, I cast my care on Thee;
>   I triumph and adore;
> Henceforth my great concern shall be
>   To love and please Thee more.
>   *John Ryland*

Or take another hymn:

> Teach me to love Thee as Thine angels love,
>   One holy passion filling all my frame;
> The baptism of the Heaven descended Dove,
> My heart an altar, and Thy love the flame.
>   *George Croly*

So there are the lessons of this first miracle performed by our Lord in Cana of Galilee. It is a picture which opens our eyes to the possibilities of the glorious fullness of the Christian life, this life which is life indeed, life more abundant. It is life developing and increasing until we find ourselves face to face with him, knowing no longer in part, but knowing even as we are already known, and filled and glorified and made like unto him. May God by his Spirit give us the understanding to realise that this is Christianity and all this is meant for us.

6

The Cleansing of the Temple

And the Jews' passover was at hand, and Jesus went up to Jerusalem, and found in the temple those that sold oxen and sheep and doves, and the changers of money sitting: and when he had made a scourge of small cords, he drove them all out of the temple, and the sheep and the oxen; and poured out the changers' money, and overthrew the tables; and said unto them that sold doves, Take these things hence; make not my Father's house an house of merchandise. And his disciples remembered that it was written, The zeal of thine house hath eaten me up. John 2:13–17

At times, we all have in our minds and on our hearts the whole state and condition of the world in which we find ourselves, and this is inevitable and right.[1] The Christian faith is not a fairytale. It is not something that ignores the world. It is always practical. So we are

---

[1] This sermon was preached on Remembrance Sunday 1965.

conscious that we are in a world of crisis, a world of trouble. We are again reminded of the precarious nature of any peace that we may be enjoying as we find ourselves once more confronted by conflict, a conflict so far only in the realm of ideas, but one which may become physical at any moment.[2] And so we are reminded that that is the sort of world in which we live: a world of wars, a world of strife, a world of bloodshed.

The great question for us, of course, is: What is the message of the Christian church? What has the church to say? What is the message of the Bible in the light of all this? We are still in this world and we still have to share the vicissitudes to which the whole of the human race is heir. But there is a difference about us, we have a different view of all things, and our business is to discover exactly what it is we should be thinking and saying to our neighbours who are outside Christ and outside the church.

Now there is no difficulty about answering that question – it is all perfectly clear. We claim that the Bible alone gives us an understanding of why things are as they are. There is no other explanation of the world and its condition apart from that which is given in this book. We know perfectly well, as a purely historical fact, that the confident, optimistic speeches of statesmen and others, particularly in the nineteenth century, have been entirely falsified, and likewise those of the statesmen of the twentieth century. We know that the same

---

[2] In November 1965 the white community in Southern Rhodesia refused to accept rule by the black majority and made an illegal unilateral declaration of independence.

can be said about the philosophers with their idealistic philosophies and their theory of evolution and advance. How ridiculous it all looks when we are faced by global troubles! And it is the same with the humanists and others who repose their ultimate faith in humanity.

What do we say as Christians? What does the Bible say to all who believe it? I want to try to show you how the answer is given in these words from John's Gospel. In John's account of the cleansing of the Temple, an explanation is given, and the only solution to the problem is presented to us.

The answer is all in one blessed person. *He* is the answer to everything. It is his arrival that makes the difference. The great turning-point of history is the point at which he came into this world. That marks the end of one age and the beginning of another. It is 'the fulness of the time' (Galatians 4:4). It is in his coming into the world, in all he did while he was here, and all he has continued to do ever since that we have the key to the problem. He is, in and of himself, the one and only solution.

But I must hasten to add that it is very important that we should listen to him as he is, that we should allow him to speak to us. Many have gone astray and have failed to realise the blessings and the benefits of the Christian life just because they fail to listen to him. That, I want to suggest to you, is the main trouble at the present time. Instead of allowing him to speak, people are speaking. They are importing their own ideas into his teaching. They are twisting and perverting his teaching. They are so anxious to speak that they borrow some ideas from him and imagine that that is

Christianity. And thereby, of course, they miss the blessing.

In the Gospels it can be seen very clearly that when he arrives he always controls the entire situation. We have been studying the marriage feast at Cana of Galilee where we see trouble and confusion, no wine and nothing to be done. Then he begins to act, and the problem is solved. The answer is all and always in him. He commands the situation. He speaks, and the essence of wisdom, I say, is to listen to him. This is the supreme need of the world. There is literally no hope anywhere else.

One of the first things we must realise is that there are many sides to him. And it is partly because people do not realise this that they go astray. They always try to make him in their own image. Some emphasise one side and some another. Some stress only his death upon the cross, which to them is the supreme illustration of pacifism. Others dwell on the aesthetic aspect of our Lord, while some emphasise, over much perhaps, the stern aspect. What I am concerned to stress is that we must take him as he is and must not try to confine him to certain points of view. He breaks through the narrow limits that people have always tried to impose upon him.

Now here, in an interesting and dramatic manner, that point is brought out to us. We were looking at him in the marriage feast at Cana of Galilee, and there, on that festive occasion, he supplies the wine. What a happy picture it is! We have seen how it teaches us about the fullness of the blessing that he has to give to those who, truly seeing their need, fall at his feet and do everything that he tells them to do and wait upon him. Oh the blessedness and the happiness of that picture!

But this is what I read here: 'And when he had made a scourge of small cords, he drove them all out of the temple, and the sheep, and the oxen; and poured out the changers' money, and overthrew the tables; and said unto them that sold doves, Take these things hence; make not my Father's house an house of merchandise.' Now this is a very different picture, is it not? There is a striking contrast, but it is the same person.

John the Baptist himself saw it all, and summed it up in one striking statement. When the people were beginning to think that he, John, was the Christ, he denied it, and said, 'I indeed baptize you with water; but one mightier than I cometh, the latchet of whose shoes I am not worthy to unloose: he shall baptize you with the Holy Ghost and with fire' (Luke 3:16). There it is in those words – 'the Holy Ghost! Fire!' The blessings of the fullness, the baptism of the Holy Spirit, how wonderful, how glorious! But do not forget, there is also fire. Then John goes on to say: 'Whose fan is in his hand, and he will throughly purge his floor, and will gather the wheat into his garner; but the chaff he will burn with fire unquenchable' (verse 17).

This is where the twentieth century in particular has gone so sadly astray. Our Lord has been regarded only as the Prince of Peace; we have forgotten that he is also the King of Righteousness. And he insists upon both. He is the complete Saviour of the world, and, I repeat, the essence of wisdom is to fall at his feet, and to look to him and listen to what he has to say to us. Never did

the church and the world need to listen more atten-
tively. Do not forget the world in which you are living.
Look at it fairly, straightly. Do not blink at anything.
Do not cover over anything.

And what is the message that the world needs to
hear? Let me first put it negatively. The message of the
Lord and his word is not some general, sentimental
thought. There are people who would sentimentalise
him. Normally, they only think of him on certain occasions, and then they are only looking for some vague,
general, sentimental message of comfort. Of course he
has comfort – but it is his comfort; it is his peace. He
says, 'Peace I leave with you, my peace I give unto you:
not as the world giveth, give I unto you. Let not your
heart be troubled, neither let it be afraid' (John 14:27).
He does not offer a peace that the world knows about.
His peace is a peace which always has in it the element
of righteousness and justice and truth. It is not merely
the absence of war. Nor is it some vague, general talk
about sacrifice and the value of sacrifice. Sacrifice is a
great and a wonderful and a noble thing but not as the
world uses it. So often the gospel is perverted into a
worldly kind of message on sacrifice and duty and
courage. These things are all right in their place but
they are never to be elevated to the supreme position.
And we are not interested in any idea of sacrifice, nor
duty, nor courage which is not derived directly from
the teaching of the Son of God.

Neither is the gospel a message of advice to statesmen and to leaders. That is not the preacher's calling,
that is not my business. The church is not here to tell
statesmen what to do. She has a much bigger, a much

deeper, calling, as I shall show you. So we do not spend our time in expressing our opinions as to what should be happening in political crises, and so divide the church, some saying this and some saying that. Nor is it the preacher's task to appeal to world leaders to make peace and banish war. There will always be wars and rumours of wars. No – the preacher proclaims the truth.

Well, then, what is the gospel message? It is a radical message. It is a message that proclaims the only hope and the only way of salvation. It is exactly what our Lord did when he went up to the Passover at Jerusalem, and it is interesting that this incident comes here, at the very beginning of John's Gospel, at the beginning of our Lord's ministry. This is a most significant happening, one of the crucial events in his earthly life and ministry.

In the cleansing of the Temple we see our Lord giving the Jewish nation a final warning. He is giving them an indication that unless they do what he has come to tell them to do, they are finished. In effect, he is saying: 'Listen to my words and put them into practice, or be prepared for AD 70.' And in AD 70, you remember, the Roman legions came and sacked the city of Jerusalem, destroyed the Temple, and threw out the Jews among the nations. Here our Lord is showing the only way to avoid that catastrophe.

A great deal of our Lord's ministry was devoted to that. He presented the Jews with this one possibility, this only hope, and if they rejected this, then nothing remained but nemesis. So at the end of his ministry he stood over the city of Jerusalem and said: 'O Jerusalem,

Jerusalem ... how often would I have gathered thy children together, even as a hen gathereth her chickens under her wings, but ye would not!' (Matthew 23:37).

Here, then, is his message, and it is still his message today. So I want to show you what it is. Far from being a message from church leaders to the statesmen to tell them what they must do in the realm of the state, it is primarily a message to Christian people and their leaders to tell them what they must do in their own realm, the church. For it is the tragedy of the hour that the church is telling the world what to do when the question is: Is the church in a fit condition to do so? I suggest that it is not surprising that the world does not listen.

The first emphasis of the Christian message is that the supreme matter in the life of an individual or a nation is each person's relationship to God. And all this is typified by the Temple. The Temple, after all, was the greatest and the grandest of all the palaces and for-tifications in Jerusalem. The Jews were the people of God, and it was there they went to worship him and to meet with him. It was the centre of the life of the nation. That is why our Lord not only went to the Temple on this occasion but behaved in the manner that he did and said what he said.

If you read the story of the Children of Israel in the Old Testament, you will find that when things were right in the Temple, and when the Children of Israel were loyal to God, all went well with them in every other respect – in war, in material prosperity, and so on. But the moment there was a declension in the temple worship, deterioration invariably followed in

the life of the people: like priests, like people. This runs
as a kind of theme through the whole of the Old Testament. So here our Lord is, as it were, summing it all
up, pointing out that this is still relevant, that the laws
of God do not change, and that this is the people's only
way of safety and of security and peace.

There are many glowing phrases in the Old Testament which sum this all up. Here are some of them:
'Where there is no vision, the people perish' (Proverbs
29:18). It does not matter how wealthy they are nor
what their armaments are, 'Where there is no vision
. . .' It is this that controls everything else. History
shows that it is possible for a people, a nation, to ride
for quite a long time on the vision of those who went
before them. Nemesis does not come at once. There is
a gradual decline and fall. But once the vision has been
lost, you can expect what we are getting today.

Take another verse: 'Righteousness exalteth a nation'
(Proverbs 14:34). Not possessions, not wealth, not
material power, but 'righteousness'. And when a
nation, or any individual, is righteous, these other
things follow. Our Lord summed it all up in one phrase
in the Sermon on the Mount: 'Seek ye first the kingdom of God, and his righteousness; and all these things
shall be added unto you' (Matthew 6:33).

Perhaps the most striking illustration is the story of
the high priest, Eli, which we read in 1 Samuel. Eli was
a good man but he was too soft, too indulgent. He
allowed his feelings and temperament to guide him
rather than the Law of God. His two sons were evil
men – in 1 Samuel 2 you can read how they abused
their office. The poor old man was too weak to stop

them, so they went on, fattening themselves on their
holy office, and living immoral and unworthy lives.
There we see decline starting in the house of God, but
it soon followed in the whole of the nation. The Philistines came and Israel was ignominiously defeated. The
Philistines even carried away the very ark of God.

That is typical of the message in the Old Testament,
and now here it is in the New. When things go wrong
in the Temple they will go wrong everywhere. The key
to everything is our relationship to God.

That, then, is the controlling principle, and then the
second follows of necessity. I am just expounding what
we read here in John 2:13–17: our greatest danger of all
is to misunderstand and abuse the means of grace
which God has given us to strengthen our individual
worship and walk with him. We use them to suit our
own ends and our own purposes. This is the great lesson
of the Children of Israel put before us in a very dramatic
manner here and, later, by the events of AD 70. The
trouble with the Jews was always that they misused and
misappropriated what God had given to them. As our
Lord shows here, they abused the Temple. Not only
was this their trouble, it was the cause of their final
tragedy.

And I solemnly suggest to you that the explanation
of the state of many countries in the world at this hour
is the abuse or misuse of the 'temple', the misappropriation of the things that God has given us and their use
for our own unworthy and selfish ends. That is always
the cause of the trouble, and eventually it is not only a
wrong but a mad thing to do.

What am I talking about? Well so often in Israel the

first thing that went wrong when they lost the living
Spirit was that they turned the temple worship into
something formal and external. There is nothing more
terrible in the life of an individual or a nation than a
formal religion, just going through the movements
when it suits you, without any feeling, any spirit, any
real belief; just going to church because it is the thing to
do, and a nice thing to do, perhaps, on certain occasions. The formalising and externalising of religion is a
great curse. And not only does the history of the Children of Israel demonstrate that, if you read the subsequent history of the Christian era, you will find
exactly the same thing.

What is extraordinary in this incident in John 2 is
that the presence of these oxen, and sheep, and doves,
and the changing of money was not wrong in and of
itself, it was necessary. People came up to Jerusalem to
these feasts from a great distance and they could not
bring these animals up with them all the way. So it was
quite legitimate that there should be men selling oxen,
sheep and doves. And, again, there were people who
had come from different parts of the world with their
different coinage and so you had to have money-
changers. There was nothing wrong in all this.

This is what was wrong: the buying and selling had
come right into the Temple and for many people had
become their main purpose in being there. Men were
becoming fat on the money they made. Our Lord was
concerned about the misuse of that which was right and
appropriate. God has appointed the way of worship
and has indicated it to us. In the Old Testament era he
instituted the external rituals of the Temple and its

ceremonial; we now worship him in a more internal, spiritual manner. But the principle is the same and God has ordained these things.

Here lies the danger, it is the danger of taking these things that God himself has appointed for us and using them to serve our own ends, using them in our way, using them to further our own interests. That is what our Lord turns against in this drastic, majestic manner.

Let us be practical about this. Are you really concerned about the state of the world? If you are, this is no time for sentimentality, this is a time for listening to the Son of God, for hearing his message. And I believe he is speaking in an unusually clamant manner in these days, especially in view of what has been happening recently in Southern Rhodesia. This has not occurred in the history of this country since 1776. It is a very serious matter. It is indicative of something profound that is taking place, and I suggest to you that a major cause has been the use for our own ends of what God has appointed, especially in his church and in his worship. It is using the church as a part of the national life, almost as a department of the state, a backdrop for great occasions and for births, marriages and deaths. The ceremonial of the church, given by God, is appropriated for our own ends and purposes. So, for example, Christian memorial services are held for men and women who are unbelievers and well-known scoffers at the Christian faith. The state's use of the church in this way, and the church's willingness to be used, are abuses of what God has given.

Is this important? Well, I suggest to you it is as important as this: it provides the reason why some countries today are nominally atheistic. In these countries, the state and the church were so identified that when the people wanted a change in the state, the church was involved. It was the association between the Russian royal family and the Russian Orthodox Church, especially as represented by that fiend Rasputin, that accounted for the revolution in Russia. The people abominated the church. They said that if that was Christianity, they did not want it. That was why they turned to atheistic Communism. And France did the same at the time of the French Revolution.

Now all this has surely a great deal to say to us. Can the British people plead guiltless to the charge of having used the Christian church as a part of colonial policy? Now this is important because the countries we used to call the Colonies are becoming independent nations and in many we are seeing a repetition of the same story. They have identified colonial policy with Christianity. Church and state have gone together. The sword and the bishop, as it were, are intertwined, and when one is rejected, so is the other. These issues are vital and very solemn. If the church is used as a part of colonial policy, or as a part of an attempt to impose western civilisation upon other countries, then when there is a rebellion against western civilisation, the church will go out with it. We are reaping what we have sown and must not be surprised at the result.

Then there was the danger, especially in the First World War, of using the church as a kind of glorified recruiting station. The Christian message was turned into appeals for heroism and sacrifice and courage in the interests of the state. It is not surprising that the masses of the people are outside the Christian church. Men and women are not fools. They observe these things, and many have reacted violently because of what took place in the First World War.

But apart from all that, there are many who have used the church, and still do, simply to propagate human theories and teachings. Some even advocate Communism in the name of Christianity. They push forward their own philosophies, always preaching politics, dealing with material matters, but using the Scriptures, using the terminology, evacuating it of its true meaning and using it to serve their own ends. Moreover, the church has often been foolish enough to allow herself to be used by culture. Many people go to church services only to listen to the music and are not interested in anything else. And the church has allowed herself to be used for the sake of music or the sake of art and so on. Others have used the church to serve their own personal ambition, seeking a career and worldly advancement. How often has it been said in the past that in the great landed families the eldest son went to the navy, the second to the army, and then down the line somewhere a younger son entered the church?

But all this is sheer misappropriation. Here we see the sheep and the oxen and the doves and the money-changers. And this is why the masses of the people are outside the Christian church. They have said, 'If that is Christianity, we are not interested in it.'

So the story of our Lord in the temple court is still relevant, is it not? It is our Lord who throws out the sheep and pigeons and the money-changers. I am not expressing my own opinions here. We are studying his actions when he went up to the Passover at Jerusalem.

So my next principle is that the supreme need of this hour is for men and women to know the presence of the Lord in power in the church. That is why I am not preaching about Southern Rhodesia. The need is not for something to happen in the state, but for something to happen in the church. Why are the statesmen ignoring the church? Because the church has no power. There have been times when statesmen have had to listen to the church: think of John Knox preaching and Mary Queen of Scots sitting trembling as she listened. That is the right order. But that only happens when Christ is present in the Temple in power. So as we look out at the world remembering two world wars and all their devastation, seeing what is happening to men and women who are suffering in many places, seeing the dread possibilities in the world, I say that the message that is needed is the message that comes when Christ enters into the Temple and begins to speak and to act. And, therefore, if you and I are genuinely concerned about the world and its state, our first duty is to pray for revival in the church. It is not to say things to the world, but to seek this power which will enable us to speak to the world in such a manner that it will tremble as it listens to us.

Next we must see what he does when he comes. 'The Jews' Passover was at hand, and Jesus went up to Jerusalem' – and things began to happen. And what do we find? At once we see the manifestation of his glory, of his authority, of his zeal, of his power. Had you realised, when you had read this incident, that it is a miracle? It is as much a miracle as the changing of the water into wine at the marriage feast of Cana of Galilee. Look at these men: wealthy, astute men, clever men, here they are trading in the Temple, and yet this defenceless person makes a kind of whip out of cords and with that alone drives them out, together with their sheep and their cattle. He turns to the men who have the doves, and says, 'Take these things hence.' And he overturns the tables of the money-changers, and pours out their money.

But how can a thing like this happen with just this one person, armed only with a whip of small cords? There is only one answer: it is the manifestation of his glory, just as at the marriage feast. We read there, you remember, 'This beginning of miracles did Jesus in Cana of Galilee, and manifested forth his glory.' His word has power. He is the Son of God in the flesh. He speaks authoritatively, and men feel it instinctively.

We find this happening many times in the pages of the four Gospels. When he speaks, or even looks at men and women, they slink out. They cannot face him. They cannot stand it. He is the Son of God, supreme in authority and power. And that is why we should pray for this power to be known today. It is he who has constituted us, it is he who alone can enable us, and he has promised to do so. Our greatest need is that in him, and in his strength, we may speak with a like authority.

In this incident we find that our Lord acts as he always does. He pronounces and executes judgement. He looks at all this: '[He] found in the temple those that sold oxen and sheep and doves, and the changers of money sitting . . .' And he looks with indignation. The zeal of his Father's house has eaten him up. He is filled with a holy sense of righteousness, so he pronounces judgement upon it all. And if you are not conscious of God pronouncing judgement upon the Christian church at the present time, I almost despair. Can you not hear it? Can you not feel it? Can you not see it? Why this utter confusion? Why do the common people in all countries find the church almost fatuously ridiculous? It is God's judgement. God is ridiculing the church because of the abuse and the misuse of which we have all been so guilty.

And what else? Well, our Lord institutes reform. He clears out those things that do not belong there. And, I repeat, the supreme need at the present hour is reform of the Christian church, reform of her doctrine, a casting away of all the accumulation of sheer paganism. Listen to his words. He says, 'Take these things hence.' All your trappings and paraphernalia, all your incense and attempts at burnt offerings and sacrifices, all your masses, must be thrown out. He always throws them out. There must be reformation: a reformation in doctrine, a getting rid of all the superstition, all the lies. All that makes men great and important and hides him and his eternal glory has to go. This is what happened at the Protestant Reformation and it happens at every other period of reformation and of revival. He clears out the false, in doctrine, in practice, and in behaviour. And then what does he do? He restores the original simplicity.

Later on our Lord has to say something very similar because they did not pay attention to him. At the end of his ministry he tells them that they have turned his Father's house into a den of thieves (Matthew 21:13). But it is meant to be a house of prayer! The business of the church is to bring men and women to God and to keep them in communion with him. The church should be filled with such power from God that everybody, in a sense, will be forced to listen. The moment you simplify your religion, the power increases. These other things – the false in doctrine, the false in practice – hide the truth from the masses of the people, and they must be cleared out. We must return to that simplicity which is in Christ Jesus.

And when you do that, what happens? Go back and read your history, read about the Protestant Reformation. What did it lead to? Well, among other things, it led to the Elizabethan period.

It was exactly the same in the Puritan era. You can laugh at the Puritans if you like, but never forget that the Cromwellian period, the period of the Commonwealth, was one of the greatest periods in the whole history of England and Wales. Everybody is agreed, even secular historians, that the basis of this country's greatness was laid down then, when there was a moral tone in the nation, and men and women put God first. Then the whole nation was elevated: 'Righteousness exalteth a nation' (Proverbs 14:34).

It is in a large measure true to say that what was truly great and glorious in the nineteenth century was the direct outcome of the Evangelical Awakening of the eighteenth century. This can be established historically. One historian tells us that it was that, and that alone, that saved this country from something similar to the French Revolution. Other historians confirm that the Evangelical Awakening was the origin, not only of greatness in a national sense, but of the enlightenment of the people.

The Trade Union movement, for example, came directly out of this revival. Everything that elevates men and women, everything that makes them realise who and what they are, everything that reminds them that they have minds and inspires them to learn and to get on, it all comes out of the original blessing of hearkening to the Son of God and allowing him to deal with the church, and to deal with us as individuals.

Once the centre is made right, once the Temple is cleansed and reformed and renewed, the change percolates through the whole of life and there is a new tone. Where there is no vision, the people perish. Where there is vision, the people succeed. And this is the supreme need of the present hour. Our need is to recapture the vision, to turn back to him, allow him to act and to speak to us, to cleanse and to drive out.

So there, it seems to me, is the message of the Bible to this world. Oh that this Christ would come and again make his scourge and upset and overturn and drive out and cleanse, and give us to know once more in simplicity and in purity his faith, and the power that comes inevitably to all who believe in him and who submit to him, and want to be filled with his blessed Holy Spirit. Oh that he would come again to the Temple! Let us begin to offer that prayer. Pray for others – all right, but that is not the *first* prayer. The first prayer is not prayer for statesmen, nor for friends or relatives, nor for other nations, that is not the *first* prayer. The first prayer is to plead with him to come into his Temple, to manifest his glory, to show us something of the might of his power and to fill us with that power.

7

The Temple of the Living God

And the Jews' passover was at hand, and Jesus went up to Jerusalem, and found in the temple those that sold oxen and sheep and doves, and the changers of money sitting: and when he had made a scourge of small cords, he drove them all out of the temple, and the sheep and the oxen; and poured out the changers' money, and overthrew the tables; and said unto them that sold doves, Take these things hence; make not my Father's house an house of merchandise. And his disciples remembered that it was written, The zeal of thine house hath eaten me up. John 2:13–17

We have looked at the cleansing of the Temple in a general manner in terms of the message that it has to give to the church as a whole. But obviously, and as commentators throughout the centuries have agreed, this is equally a message for the individual Christian. We have seen how the people obeyed our Lord immediately when he told them to go, and we realised

that the only explanation for that is that they were
made conscious of something of his eternal power and
Godhead. So we must bear that in mind now as we
come to apply the message of this incident to ourselves.

As I have said, my fundamental proposition is that
the great theme of John's Gospel is that 'He came that
we might have life, and that we might have it more
abundantly'. And I am suggesting that every one of
these dramatic incidents in John's Gospel gives us some
further aspect of the teaching concerning the way in
which he will give us this great blessing of his fullness.

It is important, therefore, that we should remember
that we must take him as he is. He is 'the Lord'. It is he
who acts; it is he who decides how to act. The question
that I want to put to you now is this: Have we received
of his fullness, and grace upon grace? We must always
ask ourselves this question, because all his actions can
only be understood and interpreted in the light of that.
All he did and said is an indication of what is essential
before we can come to that fullness, and here he shows
us, in a clear and definite manner, one of the conditions.

You remember that it is the time of the Passover, and
our Lord has gone up to Jerusalem, as the Law commands all Jews to do. We see him arriving in the Temple
and we are told what he finds there. In that outer court
merchants are selling oxen and sheep and doves, and
money-changers are exchanging foreign currency for
temple coins. The whole place fills our Lord with a
sense of horror. He upsets the tables of the money-
changers, throwing them and the sheep and the oxen
out, and he commands the people with the doves, 'Take
these things hence.' He, as it were, purges the Temple.

What, then, is the teaching? What is the message that we receive here as individuals? Let me put it to you like this: our souls are temples into which our Lord comes to dwell. That is our basic and fundamental proposition. That is the ultimate in this matter of Christian salvation. Christian salvation does not only mean that we are forgiven, it is not simply that we are assured that we do not go to hell because God has forgiven us our sins. Nor does it only mean that we receive a new nature. These things are glorious and all-important and we thank God for them. But Christian salvation offers us something beyond that, and that is – and this is the astounding thing – nothing less than the Lord Jesus Christ dwelling in us. This is a picture that we find in many places in the Bible. Indeed, all we are told in the Old Testament about the Temple should not only teach us about the church in general and about how to worship in the house of God, but should give us a picture of the individual soul.

Later on in John's Gospel this truth is put before us quite plainly and explicitly. Our Lord is reminding his disciples that he is going to leave them, but he adds that he will not leave them comfortless. He says, 'At that day ye shall know that I am in my Father, and ye in me, and I in you. He that hath my commandments, and keepeth them, he it is that loveth me; and he that loveth me shall be loved of my Father, and I will love him, and will manifest myself to him' (John 14:20–21). Then in verse 23 we read, 'Jesus answered and said unto him, If a man love me, he will keep my words: and my Father will love him, and we will come unto him, and make our abode with him.' Now that is the fullness of the

Christian experience. God's ultimate purpose is that he should dwell in men and women: 'the life of God in the soul of man', as Henry Scougal put it.

Take the way Paul expresses this in 2 Corinthians. Having asked the question 'What agreement hath the temple of God with idols?', he reminds his readers of the great promise: 'for ye are the temple of the living God; as God hath said, I will dwell in them, and walk in them; and I will be their God, and they shall be my people' (2 Corinthians 6:16). And in 1 Corinthians, he says, 'Know ye not that your body is the temple of the Holy Ghost which is in you' (1 Corinthians 6:19). This is the ultimate which we should always keep in our minds with regard to our faith. As we saw in the last study, Paul's prayer for the Ephesians is 'That he [God] would grant you, according to the riches of his glory, to be strengthened with might by his Spirit in the inner man; that Christ may dwell in your hearts by faith . . .' (Ephesians 3:16–17). Paul is writing to Christian people, but he is praying for them that they may go on to know this.

We must never be content with anything less in the Christian life. We must learn to regard our souls as temples in which God comes to dwell: God the Father, God the Son, and God the Holy Spirit. We notice that this teaching is always given as Christians are being led forward to realise all that is possible for them as believers in Christ Jesus.

So, having started with the proposition that each of us is the temple of God, the next question we have to face is this: What is the condition of these temples? And here we see the relevance to us of this incident in the Temple at Jerusalem. Now let me make it quite clear that I am not concerned at this point with those who are not Christians. I am speaking specifically and definitely to Christian people. Our Lord is in the Temple, the Temple that God had given to the Children of Israel. He is not dealing here with Gentiles, but with Jews. He is dealing with religious people, with God's own people. It is important to bear that in mind because otherwise we shall miss the whole point of this incident. We are very ready to see that certain things must be done to the unbeliever, but here we are concerned with what must be done, and what the Lord will do, with believers, in order that he may come and dwell in their hearts by faith. And so we must examine the Temple, exactly as our Lord did on this occasion when he went up to Jerusalem at the time of the Passover feast.

An old Puritan put this matter very clearly in a graphic analogy. Talking primarily about the unregenerate, he said that the condition of men and women in sin and as the result of the fall is similar to the state of many an old castle up and down the country. You find the castle in ruins, overgrown with thorns and briars and nettles, but if you look carefully you often see a notice which reads something like this: 'Once upon a time so-and-so dwelt here.' That castle was the ancestral home of some great person. And the old Puritan said that that is the sort of notice that you find written on the soul of every unbeliever: 'God once dwelt here.' But no longer: it is ruined; it is broken down. The walls and battlements have all fallen to the ground and are so overgrown that you can scarcely recognise them. You scarcely recognise that there ever was a place of habitation there. That is the unbeliever, but we are concerned with the believer, and the question is: What do we find in this temple?

And the message is surely that the condition of the soul of so many believers is very similar to that of the Temple in Jerusalem. Here is God's house, with all its ceremonies appointed and ordained by God himself, but our Lord finds an abuse of all this. The place is being used to serve men's own selfish ends, and activities which are quite legitimate in and of themselves – buying and selling cattle and sheep and doves, and money changing – have been turned into the big thing, the main thing. So our Lord can sum it up by saying that they have made his Father's house 'an house of merchandise'. And here each of us is called upon to examine the state of our own soul, this place in which God wills to dwell.

What is the condition of our soul as our Lord examines it at this moment? What is to be found there? He looks upon it all – what does he see? Does he see sin? Does he see evil? Does he see things taking place which should not be there? Is there an element of unbelief? Is there an element of doubt and of uncertainty? Are there ugly and foul and unworthy things? What about the thoughts and the imaginations and the intents of the heart? These are the things which he searches out.

Now in the Old Testament we can read all the details which God commanded first to Moses, and then to David and Solomon, concerning the building of the tabernacle and the Temple, and we see that everything was designed in order to create a fit place in which God could dwell. And we must examine ourselves in the light of all this. But there is a further way in which we must examine ourselves, and this is most important of all. The chief trouble with these people was that the very things that God had appointed to them as ways and means of worship they were misusing for their own base and unworthy ends. So the important thing for us to ask ourselves is: What use are we making of the gospel of our Lord and Saviour?

We believe in the doctrine of justification by faith only, in the free forgiveness of sins. That is right, but what use are we making of it? Are we saying that therefore it does not matter what we do, that we can sin because we know we shall be forgiven? Are we making 'merchandise' of the cross of Christ? That is an expression which is used by Peter: 'with feigned words they make merchandise of you' (2 Peter 2:3). People turn the very blood and cross of Christ into personal profit.

In other words, are we saying, 'Well now, I'm a believer in the Lord Jesus Christ. I know I'll be forgiven, there's no question at all about that. Therefore I can do what I like. I only have to repent and say I'm sorry and I'll be forgiven'? If we think such things, we are trading, trading with the blood of Christ.

So this is the kind of lesson that our Lord is teaching as he makes that scourge of small cords, and drives out these people. Are we using the means of grace, the glories of the gospel, simply to ease our conscience, simply to continue in sin and avoid punishment? This is a terrible thing, and I think that as we examine ourselves we will find that we have often been guilty of it

– that we have, in this most subtle and almost devilish manner, been misappropriating for our own ends the very things that God has given us.

There are many other things about which we can examine ourselves – I am not going into details. 'Let a man examine himself.' That is Paul's instruction for us when we come to the Communion Table. Paul said this because the Corinthians were abusing the Lord's Supper. Some of them were coming to their love feasts and to the Communion Service selfishly, in order to eat and drink too much. And so we read that terrible warning: 'But let a man examine himself.' Why? Because, says Paul, whether you do or not, he will judge you. Because you do not believe as you should, 'many are weak and sickly among you, and many sleep' (1 Corinthians 11:28, 30). If you do not want to be judged and condemned with the world, examine yourselves, get rid of these things. And we must do the same, all along the line. There is nothing more terrible than to be using the means of grace, the house of God, the glories and the blessings of the gospel, to serve some personal, selfish end.

Now I know – and thank God for this – there is probably less of this now than there has been for many a long day. When it was the thing to go to the house of God, as it was a hundred or so years ago, people were much more guilty of this sin than they are now. As I was indicating in the last study, people commonly used the house of God and the means of grace to further perhaps their own business or their own career. There is not so much of that today because it is a day in which the worship of God is no longer as popular as it once was. But even today there is still the possibility that we may be using these very things that God has given us for our own base and unworthy objects. So as we examine ourselves, I am sure we are ready to cry out with him who said:

> The ruins of my soul repair,
> And make my heart a house of prayer.
>   *Charles Wesley*

But having shown you the general principle, let me go on to show you the particular things that we must realise in the light of this teaching. The first of these is his lordship. Here he is, just a carpenter from Nazareth, but he comes to the Temple and immediately takes charge. He does it as one who has a right to do so, who has the authority. It is his. He talks in verse 16 of 'my Father's house'. He does not say 'our' Father, but 'my' Father, thereby indicating that he is none other than the Son of God, and that he comes as the Lord of the Temple, as the One who has a right to it, and as the One who has a right to do whatsoever he pleases in it.

It is tragic that in evangelism a distinction is often drawn between the Lord Jesus Christ as Saviour and the Lord Jesus Christ as Lord. There is a distinction, of course, but if you press it to a division you are doing one of the most dangerous things conceivable. This happens, does it not? You are told to accept Jesus as your Saviour, and the idea is given that you can take him as your Saviour only and only later, when you are taken to a meeting, will you be presented with him as your Lord. And then you will be told, 'As you took him as your Saviour, take him now as your Lord.' As if it were possible to take him without taking him as your Lord!

One of the striking lessons in this whole incident is that we must take him as he is. And he always appears in the fullness of his blessed person. We do not believe in 'Jesus', but in the Lord Jesus Christ. We cannot divide him in this wrong sense. He insists that we take him as a whole. There is no such thing as getting the blessings of forgiveness and pardon without at the same time believing in him as Lord. He came not merely that we might be forgiven, but he 'gave himself for us, that he might redeem us from all iniquity, and purify unto himself a peculiar people, zealous of good works' (Titus 2:14). He came 'that he might bring us to God' (1 Peter 3:18). He came to make us a holy people, and no aspect of salvation must ever be isolated from that.

You say you believe in the death of Christ upon the cross for your sins. Very well, immediately you draw this deduction, then, as Paul says, 'Know ye not . . . ye are not your own? For ye are bought with a price' (1 Corinthians 6:19–20). In dying for you he 'buys' you; he has possessed you; you belong to him. He is the Lord of the Temple.

This is the first principle of the Christian life. The moment we are convicted of sin and the danger of punishment and of hell, we realise that we have been the slaves of sin and of Satan, but that now, by believing in him, we are not only forgiven, but are liberated and belong to him. We have become the bondslaves of the Lord Jesus Christ.

Oh, how much trouble we would save ourselves if

we only held that great realisation constantly in our minds! The Christian is never free – never. We are all slaves – either slaves of the devil or slaves of the Son of God. The apostle Paul glories in this title. 'Paul,' he says, 'a servant' – which means 'a bondslave' – 'of Jesus Christ' (Romans 1:1). Therefore from the very beginning, our Lord insists upon our observing this.

As we saw in the marriage feast of Cana of Galilee, he will not be dictated to. He will not even receive suggestions. He is the Lord, and he decides and determines. He does exactly the same thing in the Temple. So there must be no arguing whatsoever about this. We are his rightful possession.

The next thing that he makes quite clear is that when he comes to his possession, he will inspect it and he knows everything. Nothing can be hidden from him. Here again is a great principle that runs through the whole of the Bible, in the Old Testament as well as in the New. The classic example is poor David. David, the son of Jesse, this wonderful king of Israel, this 'sweet psalmist' – O yes, this man of God – he fell into sin. He planned it and plotted it, and he thought he had been very clever. He thought he had covered over his tracks. And, indeed, he had deceived most of the people. Only one or two people knew what he had been doing. David thought all was going to be well. But he was soon disabused of that idea. God sent the prophet Nathan to deal with him, and David's sin was exposed.

In Psalm 51 David made a complete confession and this is what he says: 'Thou desirest truth in the inward parts' (Psalm 51:6). He realised at last that God does not merely concern himself with our external actions but God knows the heart.

Again, in another psalm, David says, 'If I regard iniquity in my heart, the Lord will not hear me' (Psalm 66:18). Now to regard iniquity in the heart means to hide something, to cover it over. We say, 'I'm a Christian,' but at the same time deliberately shield just some sin.

'It is no good,' says David in effect, 'the Lord will not hear me.' God demands absolute honesty in this matter. He demands complete openness. He cannot be deceived, he cannot be fooled. God knows everything and God is everywhere.

We find the same thing in Psalm 139. The psalmist writes, 'Whither shall I flee from thy presence? If I ascend up into heaven, thou art there: if I make my bed in hell, behold, thou art there' (Psalm 139:7-8). Wherever I am – east, west, north, south – I cannot escape from God's presence. This, too, is fundamental to Christian living. The trouble, of course, with so many of us is that we think of God looking at us in terms of particular sins. But we must not. We must think in terms of relationship and understand that he knows all about us.

Perhaps the clearest statement of God's knowledge of us is in the fourth chapter of the great Epistle to the Hebrews. The writer says,

Let us labour therefore to enter into that rest, lest any man fall after the same example of unbelief. For the word of God is quick, and powerful, and sharper than any twoedged sword, piercing to the dividing asunder of soul and spirit, and of the joints and marrow, and is a discerner of the thoughts and intents of the heart. Neither is there any creature that is not manifest in his sight: but all things are naked and opened unto the eyes of him with whom we have to do.   Hebrews 4:11–13

There is also a tremendous statement of this truth at the end of Mark's Gospel. We are told that just before the end our Lord again went to the Temple in Jerusalem and just looked round 'upon all things' (Mark 11:11). And I like to think that now he is looking round the temple of your soul where nothing is hidden from his eyes. As the writer of the hymn has put it:

> Thy kind but searching glance can scan
> The very wounds that shame would hide.
> *Henry Twells*

We are dealing with a person who is *the Lord*, and who not only has the right and the authority but also complete insight, knowledge, vision, 'scanning power'.

Then the next principle is that he very soon makes clear that he hates certain things. He will not tolerate them in his house and will never dwell side by side with them. This is a great message, is it not? Is it not extraordinary how we can ever miss this truth? These are the first principles of the Christian life. There is no need to work out the great arguments about particular sins, trying to decide what is right and what is wrong. It is a question of personal relationship. If you simply think of that, most of your problems are immediately solved. It will be no use trying to pretend or explain, he is looking on, and you are doing things in his sight.

He reveals immediately what he thinks about sin.

His attitude is perfectly clear. There is something tremendous about this. It has its terrifying aspect but it is also glorious. We read in the Book of Revelation of John's vision of him. John says, 'His eyes were as a flame of fire' (Revelation 1:14). They are the eyes of love, the eyes of compassion, the eyes of the One who died for our sins but, let us never forget it, his eyes are also like a flame of fire. This is the element of judgement. It is put here in John 2 in these terms: 'The zeal of thine house hath eaten me up.'

Why did our Lord ever come from heaven? It was because he saw the ruin that men and women in sin had made of God's universe, especially of the human soul. He saw what the devil had done, the marring of the image, and his righteous soul was grieved: 'The zeal of thine house hath eaten me up.'

He is consumed with a passion for God's right and God's glory, and God's justice. And this comes out in all his dealings with us. He hates sin. 'Thou art of purer eyes than to behold evil, and canst not look on iniquity,' we are told by Habakkuk (Habakkuk 1:13). And the same thing is true of our blessed Lord himself. God dwells in this 'light which no man can approach unto' (1 Timothy 6:16). Think of Isaiah's vision in Isaiah 6: the holiness of God, and the smoke filling the house, and the posts of the door shaking. It is a vision of God and his eternal glory, and it always reveals sin and uncleanness. 'Woe is unto me,' cries Isaiah, 'for I am undone; because I am a man of unclean lips, and I dwell in the midst of a people of unclean lips' (Isaiah 6:5).

And, of course, in all his teaching our Lord shows

his condemnation of sin. He says, 'No man can serve two masters: for either he will hate the one and love the other; or else he will hold to the one and despise the other. Ye cannot serve God and mammon' (Matthew 6:24). These are absolutes and they are utter incompatibilities.

Or take that great statement of this truth by the apostle Paul in 2 Corinthians 6. Here we see a logical statement of the truth that Christ enacted in the Temple at Jerusalem. Listen to Paul's questions. Referring primarily to the issue of a Christian marrying a non-Christian, Paul says, 'Be ye not unequally yoked together with unbelievers' (2 Corinthians 6:14). 'Don't do it,' says Paul. But why not? Paul lifts the argument up into the realm of general principles and asks, 'For what fellowship hath righteousness with unrighteousness? and what communion hath light with darkness? and what concord hath Christ with Belial? or what part hath he that believeth with an infidel? and what agreement hath the temple of God with idols?' (2 Corinthians 6:14–16). These things, he says, are complete opposites. You cannot mix righteousness with unrighteousness; you cannot mix belief with unbelief. To try to do so will always precipitate disaster. By his act there in the Temple our Lord makes this perfectly plain.

James also works this out: 'Doth a fountain send forth at the same place sweet water and bitter? Can the fig tree, my brethren, bear olive berries? either a vine, figs? so can no fountain both yield salt water and fresh' (James 3:11–12). And John puts it in still stronger language when he says, 'He that saith, I know him, and

keepeth not his commandments, is a liar, and the truth
is not in him' (1 John 2:4).

In other words, the Lord Jesus Christ will not dwell
with the sheep and the oxen and the doves and the
money-changers. He will not take up his abode in a
place of riot and of foulness and uncleanness. The last
book in the Bible, the Book of Revelation, takes this
truth right up. In the final two chapters we are shown
a vision of heaven and we read, 'And there shall in no
wise enter into it anything that defileth' (Revelation
21:27). Only that which is pure and clean and holy has
a place in heaven.

So, then, what happens in the light of all this? The
answer is given here quite simply. There are two
activities – his activity and our activity. It is always the
same. 'When he had made a scourge of small cords, he
drove them all out of the temple ... And said unto
them that sold doves, Take these things hence; make
not my Father's house an house of merchandise.'

First of all – and oh, I trust this will be made plain
and clear to all of us! – when he acts in this situation, he
does things that are very surprising to many of us. We
cannot understand it, and we begin to wonder what is
happening. So often, when we realise that we are not
living the Christian life as we should, when we realise
that more is possible for us, we think that all we have
to do is tell him this, and ask him for a blessing, and we
will at once get the blessing. But that is a fallacy. Do
you know what you are likely to get? You are likely to
get scourged. If you really take these things seriously,
and long for your soul to be God's dwelling place, be
prepared for scourging. If you think you are

immediately going to be given a present and a positive answer and be filled with great joy and some wonderful ecstasy, you are making a big mistake. There will always be a clearing out first; there will be a process of terrible examination. God will reveal the hidden things of darkness. He will explore the dungeons of your soul and you will see things inside yourself that will horrify you. And you will complain. At times you will say, 'I wish I'd never sought this. This is making me miserable. Things are getting worse instead of better.'

But it is all right, it is a part of his treatment. If you are not ready for the scourging, you are certain to be disappointed and you will not go very far along this road. He always acts in this way. The moment you come to him and say, 'Yes, it is your temple, it is your right – act,' he will act in you. He will make the scourge of small cords and strike. He will clear out the refuse. He will cast down things that you have valued and loved. He will make you feel that he is against you, and that the whole position is quite hopeless. But that is his way of acting. 'For whom the Lord loveth he chasteneth, and scourgeth every son whom he receiveth' (Hebrews 12:6).

It is a terrible thing not to know the chastening of the Lord. If you do not know it, says the writer to the Hebrews, 'then are ye bastards and not sons' (Hebrews 12:8). And Hebrews goes on, 'Now no chastening for the present seemeth to be joyous, but grievous' (verse 11). But it is his work, let him go on with it. You are his temple and he knows what is right. He knows what is best. I say, therefore, that not only must we expect him even pray for him to do it, and I think this is a very good test of our position.

> Is there a thing beneath the sun
>> That strives with Thee my heart to share?
> Ah! tear it thence, and reign alone,
>> The Lord of every motion there;
> Then shall my heart from earth be free,
>> When it has found repose in Thee.
>> *Gerhard Tersteegen*
>> *Tr. John Wesley*

Here is Tersteegen, he has been treated with the scourge and now he has begun to understand God's purpose. He says: Is there anything else left that I have not seen? 'Ah, tear it thence . . .' He cannot do it, so he asks the Lord to do it. Drive it out, he says. Tear it out of me, and reign, 'the Lord of every motion there'. Have you ever cried out like that? Have you ever asked him to 'tear' certain things out of you? This is a sure sign that he has been dealing with you and that he has been using this blessed scourge in order that his house, his temple, may be cleansed.

Then he calls upon us to do certain things. He turns to the sellers of doves and says to them: 'Take these things hence.' This is a mystery. I do not pretend to understand it. Why does he not take it all out of us? But he does not! When the Children of Israel were taken from Egypt to Canaan, many of their enemies were destroyed for them. But then certain enemies were left for them to deal with and if they did not deal with them, then these enemies would remain to harm with them, then these enemies would remain to harm them. Moses says, 'They shall be like pricks in your eyes and thorns in your sides' (Numbers 33:55). The people had to do their part. God did a big thing, then they did the rest, and this seems to be a rule in all these matters.

So there is a great injunction in 2 Corinthians 7:1: 'Having therefore these promises, dearly beloved, let us cleanse ourselves from all filthiness of the flesh and spirit, perfecting holiness in the fear of God.' Or we can put it like this: he will do certain things to us, but then we always come to a point when he says, 'Behold, I stand at the door, and knock: if any man hear my voice, and open the door . . .' (Revelation 3:20). Now to use that as an evangelistic statement is to misuse the text. It is given in the context of a letter addressed to churches, to believers. After our Lord has done certain things, he says, 'I stand at the door, and knock; if any man . . . will open the door . . .' That is our part. He acts, and then he calls upon us to act. 'Perfecting holiness in the fear of God' (2 Corinthians 7:1); cleansing ourselves from all filthiness of the flesh and of the spirit. This is the way in which he prepares us.

And what does he prepare us for? Well, he is concerned to possess us wholly. He wants the temple to be as it should be, a temple meet for himself. He wants his Father's house not to be a place of merchandise, but to be a place in which his Father can dwell – oh, this is the great promise, listen to this: 'Ye are the temple of the living God; as God hath said, I will dwell in them, and walk in them; and I will be their God, and they shall be my people' (2 Corinthians 6:16).

Is the life of God in your soul? That is real Christianity. That is what Christianity is meant to be. It is not just taking a decision, believing that your sins are forgiven, and then carrying on with great activities. That is not essential Christianity. Essential Christianity is knowing that God is in your soul, and is walking about in it and dwelling in it. It is knowing that Christ eats and drinks with you. It is knowing him, whom to know is life eternal (see John 17:3). He came into the world in order that that might be the experience of every one of us. And when you realise that and begin to desire it and tell him so, then be prepared for the eyes 'like a flame of fire'. Nothing can be hidden. He will bring every wrong thing out to the light and it will have to be got rid of. He will deal with it and he will tell you what you must do. And then – and only then – will you know that he has taken up his abode in the temple and you will be assured that Christ is dwelling in your heart by faith.

8

Seeking Signs

Then answered the Jews and said unto him, What sign shewest thou unto us, seeing that thou doest these things? Jesus answered and said unto them, Destroy this temple, and in three days I will raise it up. Then said the Jews, Forty and six years was this temple in building, and wilt thou rear it up in three days? But he spake of the temple of his body. When therefore he was risen from the dead, his disciples remembered that he had said this unto them; and they believed the scripture, and the word which Jesus had said.   John 2:18–22

We are now going to look at the sequel to the incident in which our Lord turned the money-changers and the others out of the Temple. Here we are looking at the first real clash which took place between our Lord and the religious leaders of the Jewish nation. So far they have been passive. But now they begin to speak. In the Gospels much space is taken up with accounts of the arguments and disputations that took place between our blessed Lord and the Pharisees and scribes and others. From every standpoint, therefore, this is a most important incident for us to consider together, and I want to try to show you that it has an urgent lesson to give to the church of God at this present time.

Now let us be clear about the setting. Here we are given an account of the reaction of the Jewish leaders to the incident in the Temple. Undoubtedly these are some of the same people whom he turned out. They observed the way in which, after entering the Temple and looking round, he made this scourge of small cords, and proceeded to drive out the animals and money-changers. So they turn to him and say, 'What sign shewest thou unto us, seeing that thou doest these things?' – 'Look here,' they say in effect, 'you come here to the Temple, and you are not one of the priests, but you do not hesitate to take upon yourself the authority to do what you have just done. You are claiming that you are the Lord and the Master of the Temple. Now,' they say, 'if you are making such a claim, then you must substantiate it. Give us some proof of your authority. Give us some tangible, visible demonstration of the fact that you are entitled to do this.' The Jews use this word 'sign', you notice. 'What sign shewest thou unto us . . .' They are asking for something striking, some portent, something unusual, something that they can see.

Observe the way in which our Lord deals with their request. Here, at the start of his ministry, we see him laying down the principles on which he always acts. He does not answer them directly. They say, 'What sign shewest thou unto us?' and he replies, 'Destroy this temple, and in three days I will raise it up.' They do not understand this indirect approach. There is a hidden meaning which they miss altogether. The two points, therefore, that I want to note here are just these: our Lord's reply is indirect, and it is a prophecy of his own resurrection, as John makes clear to us: 'He spake of the temple of his body.'

Those, then, are the facts, but why did this ever happen, and what is its significance for us? The first answer is that it has a very special significance for the Jewish nation and their religious teachers and leaders. Our Lord is telling them something about themselves. He is doing in words what he has already done in action. He is showing the position at which they have arrived in their relationship to God and is thus condemning them. But I am concerned that we should see the significance of this to us today. 'All Scripture is given by inspiration of God and is profitable . . .' writes Paul to Timothy (2 Timothy 3:16). And he says of the Children of Israel in the wilderness, 'Now all these things happened unto them for ensamples, and they are written for our admonition, upon whom the ends of the world are come' (1 Corinthians 10:11). So our Lord's conversation with the Jews has its immediate local meaning but it also has a larger significance. Our Lord is here giving us his teaching concerning the whole matter of signs. The Jews lead him to do that, of course, by demanding a sign, and he deals with their question.

But how is this significant to us? Well, in this way: we are told here why it is that many people are never truly blessed by the Lord – and remember, we are dealing here with religious people. They face him in exactly the same way as everybody else, they face the same gracious invitations and offers of the gospel, but they never receive them. Here we are given one of the reasons.

Let me also remind you that we are concentrating on the great theme of the Gospel of John, summed up in our Lord's words: 'I am come that they might have life, and that they might have it more abundantly' (John 10:10). Why is it that some people never know anything about this fullness of life? And I suggest that here in this incident we are given a further answer to that question. We have already seen certain answers in the incident of the marriage feast at Cana of Galilee; here the theme is taken forward.

Now this is a subtle matter and it involves a problem. Nevertheless, it is vital because many people have gone astray over the whole question of signs and the desire for signs. That was partly the trouble with the church at Corinth, and in the subsequent history of the church we see many illustrations of the same problems.

The remarkable thing – and this is the difficulty – is that people have often started in the right way and then gone wrong. The fact that you start in the right way does not mean that you are guaranteed to continue like that. The devil is always waiting to confuse and muddle us. He wants to destroy God's work. He can turn himself into an angel of light. He can produce counterfeits. In a very subtle way, he can insinuate his own thinking, and what starts correctly can end by being terribly wrong. The church at Corinth was the church of God at Corinth, and they are all described as saints, yet they found themselves in a state of confusion. So though it is not easy, it behoves us to consider this teaching closely and carefully.

Now because of the importance of this subject of signs a great deal of attention is paid to it in the pages of the New Testament. Our Lord was constantly asked for signs. He worked miracles before the people, he did wonderful things, he uttered incomparable teaching, but they kept on bringing out the same question – 'What sign shewest thou?' For instance, we find this in John 6. Our Lord has performed the miracle of feeding the five thousand, and then the people follow him, and we are told:

> They said therefore unto him, What sign shewest thou then, that we may see, and believe thee? what dost thou work? Our fathers did eat manna in the desert; as it is written, He gave them bread from heaven to eat. Then Jesus said unto them, Verily, verily, I say unto you, Moses gave you not that bread from heaven; but my Father giveth you the true bread from heaven. For the bread of God is he which cometh down from heaven, and giveth life unto the world. John 6:30–33

This is the indirect answer again, the reference to something concerning himself which they entirely fail to grasp.

The most extended treatment of this whole matter is found in Matthew 12 where we have the best exposition you will ever find of the verses that we are now considering – and I will be looking at this chapter in more detail later on in this study. Another illustration of this comes in Matthew 16, where we read at the very beginning:

The Pharisees also with the Sadducees came [and remember, Pharisees and Sadducees were bitter enemies, they disagreed, they quarrelled, and they were at enmity with one another, but the Pharisees also with the Sadducees came], and tempting him desired him that he would shew them a sign from heaven [it is the same request]. He answered and said unto them, When it is evening, ye say, It will be fair weather: for the sky is red. And in the morning, It will be foul weather today: for the sky is red and lowring. O ye hypocrites, ye can discern the face of the sky; but can ye not discern the signs of the times? A wicked and adulterous generation seeketh after a sign; and there shall no sign be given unto it, but the sign of the prophet Jonas.   Matthew 16:1–4

Furthermore, I always feel that the story of Dives and Lazarus deals with the same theme, especially in our Lord's words at the very end. The rich man, Dives, has died and gone to hell. From hell, he begs Abraham to send the beggar Lazarus from heaven to speak to Dives' brothers: 'I pray thee therefore, father, that thou wouldest send him to my father's house: for I have five brethren; that he may testify unto them, lest they also come into this place of torment. Abraham saith unto him, They have Moses and the prophets; let them hear them. And he said, Nay father Abraham: but if one went unto them from the dead, they will repent.' In other words, you give them this spectacular sign, then they will repent and believe. 'And he [Abraham] said unto him, If they hear not Moses and the prophets, neither will they be persuaded, though one rose from the dead' (Luke 16:19–31). You see, therefore, the prominence that is given to this whole theme in the teaching of the New Testament.

So let me try to summarise the message. Obviously there is a problem in connection with the giving of signs and the demand for signs. Our Lord worked miracles in order to give signs. As we have seen, the account of the miracle of the turning of the water into wine ends: 'This beginning of miracles did Jesus in Cana of Galilee, and manifested forth his glory' – now there, you remember, 'miracles' should be translated 'signs' – 'and his disciples believed in him' (John 2:11). Our Lord gave signs in order to attest to his own person, and in order to encourage belief. Yet at the same time he condemned this request for signs, and that is where the problem arises. He gave signs, and yet when people asked for them, he would not give them. Now this is subtle and vital, and we must understand it. This is where the devil comes in and we see him acting through these Jewish leaders and others.

How do we reconcile these two positions? Well, it is quite clear from this one chapter alone that there are two main attitudes towards signs. Our Lord always causes division; he says as much: 'Think not that I am come to send peace on earth: I came not to send peace, but a sword' (Matthew 10:34). He divides between the father and the children, and the mother and her daughter, and daughter-in-law, and so on. Everything he does, he himself, his words, his actions, always cause division. That cannot be helped. Everybody must react to him, and there are only two main ways in which they can react. And, remember, our reaction to him and to what he does proclaims what we are.

Now all that is seen quite clearly in this chapter.

Here he is, he gives the signs, and you notice how the disciples react: 'His disciples believed on him.' That was at Cana of Galilee. Then when he turns those people out of the Temple the disciples react like this: 'His disciples remembered that it was written, The zeal of thine house hath eaten me up.' But the leaders of the Jews react in an entirely different manner: they are puzzled and unconvinced, and that leads them to make this request for a sign.

Is this not extraordinary? Both groups are looking at the same person, and observing the same actions, and yet the responses are entirely different. This always happens; it is happening at this present time. Let us be careful – especially in our speech. What we say proclaims what we are. Quite unconsciously we so frequently condemn ourselves.

So here are the two possible reactions, and our Lord condemns the second. They turn to him and say in effect, 'Why don't you do something visible, obvious, tangible, that will give us absolute proof? Then we'll be able to believe in you and in your authority.' But instead of a sign, our Lord gives this indirect answer, this talk concerning himself, his body, the Temple, and the forecasting of the Resurrection. The condemnation here is implicit; elsewhere it is explicit. He says, for instance, 'An evil and adulterous generation seeketh after a sign' (Matthew 12:39).

Now we must draw a distinction between this request from the Jewish leaders and the request that our Lord's mother made in Cana of Galilee. When they wanted wine, we are told: 'the mother of Jesus saith unto him, They have no wine.' And our Lord rebuked her. But she was not rebuked for the same reason as these people. Mary was asking our Lord to relieve the need. She was not asking for a miracle just in order to have a sign. She was asking for an act of compassion and of mercy and of blessing although she knew that that involved a miracle. So while she was rebuked for trying to dictate to him, she was not rebuked in the way that these Jewish leaders are on this occasion. There is a subtle difference in the two requests for a miracle.

I must also put John the Baptist into the same category as Mary. We are told that John sent two of his disciples unto our Lord: 'Now when John had heard in the prison the works of Christ, he sent two of his disciples, and said unto him, Art thou he that should come, or do we look for another?' (Matthew 11:2–3). Poor John! There he is in prison. He is an ill man, and I think he has become somewhat confused. He has already borne his great testimony to our Lord, but he cannot understand the delay. He cannot understand why our Lord is staying mainly in Galilee and spending his time among the poor people. Why does he not come down to Jerusalem and declare himself?

John receives the same indirect answer: 'Jesus answered and said unto them, Go and shew John again those things which ye do hear and see: the blind receive their sight, and the lame walk, the lepers are cleansed, and the deaf hear, the dead are raised up, and the poor have the gospel preached to them. And blessed is he, whosoever shall not be offended in me' (Matthew 11:4–6).

John is in trouble. In a sense he, too, is asking for a

sign, but not in the same spirit as these Jews. I emphasise this because the mere fact that you and I may be true Christian people does not guarantee that all our requests are always right. It is possible even for a Christian to demand signs in the wrong way. There is a right way, there is a wrong way, and that is why this matter is of such great importance for us.

So why is it that our Lord refuses this request of the Jewish leaders, here in John 2? Why does he condemn it? Here are his words – 'An evil and adulterous gener-ation seeketh after a sign' (Matthew 12:39). That is his description of the mentality that asks for signs in the wrong way. Now the word 'evil' here means an attitude which is entirely wrong, an attitude which is antagonistic, the opposite of holy. Ultimately, it means the whole state of the soul in a wrong relationship to God.

Another indication of the evil nature of this mental-ity is that it always fails to see and to understand the signs that *are* given. That is the terrible thing about this whole attitude. Look at these men here. Our Lord worked a miracle in their presence – he drove out those merchants with nothing but a scourge of small cords. As we have seen, that really was a miracle because though he was apparently just Jesus of Nazareth, the carpenter, they sensed something which made them go out. But these people do not see that. He has just worked a miracle, and yet they say: Why don't you work some striking, tremendous miracle? Then we will accept you and believe you!

Now that is always the essence of the difficulty. We read in Matthew 12 of how our Lord has just exorcised a dumb spirit or devil out of a poor devil-possessed person. He has worked a miracle before the eyes of the Pharisees and scribes, but still they go on asking for signs. They cannot see the spiritual, they cannot accept it. Because of their utter failure to see and to comprehend what is before their very eyes they are always asking for something special, dramatic, spectacular, unusual. That is a part of this evil nature.

Or to put it in another way, people who ask for signs in this wrong way are betraying a lack of true spiritual understanding; that is always the ultimate trouble. Here, for instance, our Lord answers the Jewish leaders by saying, 'Destroy this temple, and in three days I will raise it up.' But they completely misunderstand. Their reply is so typical: 'Then said the Jews, Forty and six years was this temple in building, and wilt thou rear it up in three days?' They materialise everything. They never see things spiritually. The whole characteristic of this evil outlook is that it is interested in the visible, the tangible, the physical, the material.

This lack of spiritual perception is apparent when our Lord tells a parable. The Pharisees and scribes rarely see the point. Everything is literal, and reduced to the level of this material world. In chapter 3 of John's Gospel we see that great man Nicodemus making the same mistake. Our Lord says to him, 'Except a man be born again, he cannot see the kingdom of God' (John 3:3). Out comes Nicodemus: 'How can a man be born when he is old? can he enter the second time into his mother's womb, and be born?' (John 3:4). You see, he is completely missing the spiritual point. He interprets our Lord's words in physical terms. Our Lord has to tell him: Look, I am talking about spiritual things, not things that belong to the flesh.

The apostle Paul sums up this unspiritual attitude once and for ever in 1 Corinthians 2:14: 'The natural man receiveth not the things of the Spirit of God: for they are foolishness unto him: neither can he know them, because they are spiritually discerned' (1 Corinthians 2:14). Because these people lack a spiritual understanding and apprehension, they crave for the visible and tangible: it is 'an evil generation'.

But then notice the second term in our Lord's condemnation: 'An evil and adulterous generation seeketh after a sign.' The term 'adulterous' is most significant. That is our Lord's ultimate condemnation of the Jewish nation. The prophets had often used the same language and the same imagery. Israel as a nation is the wife of Jehovah, but she is an adulterous wife, and our Lord says that this kind of generation or person is always seeking signs and portents. An adulterer is no longer content, no longer satisfied, with the marriage partner, and begins to turn away. So to be guilty of this adulterous condition means not to be content with God and his ways. This is our Lord's own description of the mentality and the spirit that craves for signs. It is 'an evil and an adulterous generation'.

This adulterous mentality is ruled by curiosity. It begins to look at others, in directions that it should not. The Children of Israel were always doing this. They were God's people and he had given them his laws. He led them along, but they were always looking at the other nations and their gods which always seemed to be much better than their own. The adulterous mentality does not keep its eyes fixed upon the Lord and his commandments and his way, but begins to be ruled by an evil curiosity. Such people tend to become interested in signs, in the spectacular, in phenomena per se, apart from their true purpose. Our Lord gives these signs, yes, but if you isolate them and separate them from him, and begin to get enraptured by them, you have already become adulterous. How subtle this matter is!

Another characteristic of the adulterous mentality is that it is guilty of lusting, that is, it has a love of sensation, and the sensational, a love of excitement, a love of something new. That is the characteristic, is it not, of every adulterous person? 'Oh, this is too tame! We want something fresh, something new, something exciting!' This is our Lord's own description of a generation of people that are always seeking after signs.

And ultimately, of course, it comes to this: animated by such a spirit, and moved and controlled by it, adulterous people eventually take their life into their own hands and decide what to do. They cannot be bothered any longer. They become impatient and take action. They take charge of each situation and make demands, and say, 'What I desire I must have.' An adulterous spirit has cravings and says that those cravings must be satisfied whatever the cost. It may involve unfaithfulness, it may involve the breaking of vows, it may involve departing from the ordained way, that does not matter. That adulterous spirit says, 'I must have it!' That is how our Lord describes the outlook and the mentality of those who are for ever seeking after signs.

Then the next point is that our Lord always refuses to grant such requests for signs. And if you think he has answered such a request from you, you are wrong. There is one who can counterfeit his actions. Our Lord does not do it here in this incident, nor in all the other incidents I have described.

But let me give you, perhaps, what is the greatest example of all. The devil put the same request to him in the temptations in the wilderness. 'If thou be the Son of God, command this stone that it be made bread' (Luke 4:3) – give me a sign. But our Lord did not do it, he refused completely and again answered the devil indirectly. It is the same with the devil's proposition to our Lord to throw himself from the pinnacle of the Temple: again this dramatic action. Give this sign, then everybody will believe in you! We see here the father of all such requests. The father of it all is always the devil. And our Lord refused his demand.

We find the same refusal at the end of our Lord's life, in his handling of King Herod. Our Lord is a prisoner and Pilate has sent him under armed guard to Herod. Herod and Pilate were enemies. They had quarrelled violently and were not speaking to one another. But now they are joined together against him. And we read in Luke 23:8–9, 'And when Herod saw Jesus, he was exceeding glad: for he was desirous to see him of a long season, because he had heard many things of him; and he hoped to have seen some miracle done by him. Then he questioned with him in many words; but he answered him nothing.' Our Lord does not answer such a man. Not only does he not work a miracle before him, he does not speak.

Again, in our Lord's trial in the presence of Pilate and the high priests, we find exactly the same thing.

They make their requests and their statements but our Lord keeps silent.

> And the high priest arose, and said unto him, Answerest thou nothing? what is it which these witness against thee? But Jesus held his peace. And the high priest answered and said unto him, I adjure thee by the living God, that thou tell us whether thou be the Christ, the Son of God. Jesus saith unto him, Thou hast said [again, you see, the indirect answer]: nevertheless I say unto you, Hereafter shall ye see the Son of man sitting on the right hand of power, and coming in the clouds of heaven.
>
> Matthew 26:62–64

And in the early hours of that morning, our Lord refuses to answer Pilate. This is an absolute rule. If we are animated by this adulterous spirit he will not grant us our requests. He has laid it down here, in the Temple at Jerusalem, at the very beginning of his ministry, and he persists right the way through to the end.

That, then, is a general exposition of the teaching of our Lord himself concerning this whole matter of asking for signs. So what are the lessons that we learn from this? First, we must ask ourselves a question: How can we know if we are guilty of spiritual adultery? Well, we must examine ourselves. We know the subtleties of our own unregenerate nature. The 'old man' has gone, but the old nature has not gone and we are still in the flesh. We know, too, the devil and his subtlety. He will do anything to ruin the testimony of the Lord Jesus Christ and rob us of his great and glorious salvation. Our Lord himself says that towards the end Satan will bring about such 'great signs and wonders; insomuch that, if

it were possible, they shall deceive the very elect'
(Matthew 24:24).

We cannot be too careful about this. The devil will
always have us go from one extreme to the other. He
will either make us altogether deny the special, glorious
blessings of the Holy Spirit, or he will drive us to
excess on the other side; and both are wrong. Here is
the teaching; here is the perfect blending. Our Lord
gives signs, but never at our request if our requests are
animated by this evil and adulterous spirit. Therefore
the first great principle is that we must make sure that
we do not have an adulterous spiritual nature within us.

As we examine ourselves, what do we look for?
Well, here is the first test: If you find in yourself any
tendency to be dissatisfied with God and his ways, be
careful. If you do not appreciate the great salvation that
you have already got, if you tend to despise it or to
speak disparagingly of it in any way, be careful. From
the very first the Christian life is always miraculous and
amazing and astounding, and should always cause us to
marvel. Any tendency, therefore, to look down upon
or to belittle any evidence of the Christian life is a
dangerous sign.

But a still more important test is this: a restless spirit.
A lusting spirit is always a sign of spiritual adultery. If
you find yourself restless and wanting excitement and
experiences, if you are always craving for them, seeking
them, and going to look for them, you are in a dangerous condition. Be careful, I plead with you in the name
of God. The Holy Spirit gives peace: 'The fruit of the
Spirit is love, joy, peace . . .' (Galatians 5:22). The
Christian should not have a restless, dissatisfied

craving. It is always a characteristic of an adulterous spirit. Be careful of becoming excited and of being in a permanent state of excitement. There is no excitement in the true experience of the Spirit. There is exhilaration, there is exaltation, there is joy, but it is entirely different from the carnal excitement which is the mark of an adulterous spirit. God preserve us from it!

But let me give you what is perhaps the greatest test of all. If you find that you are tending to allow anything at all to come before the Lord Jesus Christ in your thinking, and in your feelings, and in your desires, you are already guilty of spiritual adultery.

Now we must put this plainly. If you think more of experiences that you have had than of him, you are already wrong. The Holy Spirit was sent not to call attention to himself, but to call attention to the Lord Jesus Christ – 'He shall glorify me' (John 16:14). And if what you have had and what you have experienced does not lead you to glorify him more than you have ever done before, I suggest to you that it is a spurious experience. If you find yourself talking more about experiences, or gifts, than about him, you have already gone astray. The Spirit is given, and he does give gifts, yes, but they are all meant to lead us to bring glory to Christ in our esteem, in our talk, in our everything. The moment anything comes between us and the centrality of Christ, we have already gone astray.

Or if you find that you have become more interested in yourself and in your desires and what happens to you, than in his glory and in his praise, you are already, to put it at its very lowest, entering into a dangerous position. No, no; the Spirit is sent to glorify him. 'He

[the Spirit] shall not speak of himself [from himself] . . .
he shall glorify me' (John 16:13–14).

So, having seen the subtlety of this, having seen how
we can pass from the true to the false because of the
devil and his pressure, what do we do? Well, behave as
the disciples did. Believe what you have got; use what
has already been given to you. As Abraham said to
Dives in our Lord's parable, 'They have Moses and the
prophets.' You are wrong, says Abraham to Dives.
You say, If someone were sent to them from the dead,
then they would believe. But they would not believe.
'If they hear not Moses and the prophets, neither will
they be persuaded, though one rose from the dead'
(Luke 16:31). And they were not persuaded when our
Lord rose from the dead.

No – do not seek new experiences. Conviction is
always in terms of *truth*. 'Moses and the prophets'!
We have them. We have the Bible. So concentrate on
what he has given you. He has given the signs. The
disciples were aware of that. They saw and they
began to understand, and their faith was strengthened.
But the other people cried, 'Give us something special!'
No, no; start with what you have. Read your Scriptures, pray for enlightenment. Start with your Old
Testament – Moses and the prophets. Work through
it all. Look for him. Seek him everywhere. Come to
the Gospels. Listen to his teaching. Watch him. Follow him in the Book of Acts and go on to the Epistles.
Go down the whole history of the Christian church
and see him coming and giving the power and the signs
– but in the right way. Keep yourself to what he has
given you, and do not crave for anything outside that.

Seek our Lord always. Seek to know the Lord Jesus Christ. Seek to know his love. As long as you are seeking him, you will never go astray, but, I say again, if you begin to seek other things rather than him you will go astray. The devil, once he has got you looking in the other direction, will press you on. So keep your eye steadfast upon the Lord Jesus Christ. Tell him that you want to have all that he has to give you. Tell him that he has come to give the Spirit and say, 'I want to know you! That is what I want. I want to know your love. I do not want ecstasies as ecstasies. I do not want miracles and signs. I want to know you.'

Then submit yourself utterly and absolutely to him. It may please him to give you most amazing signs. But he decides that, not you. Do not try to dictate to him. Do not become impatient with him. Do not say, 'I must have this.' No, no, you are already wrong! Fall at his feet and wait for him. Ask, and seek, and knock, and go on doing so. Do not try to hurry him. Do not try to help him. He does not need your help, and you are opening the door to psychological methods when you try to help him in any shape or form. But keep on pleading with him. Hold on to him alone. Look only unto him and to nobody and nothing else. And in his own time and in his own way he may give you such a sign as will prostrate you to the floor and fill you with wonder and amazement, a sense of his holy, glorious person.

He may work miracles, he may do all sorts of amazing things, but he laid it down at the very beginning, in the Temple at Jerusalem, that he only does such things in his own time and in his own way, and to people who seek to know him and his glory, people who have a spiritual insight and understanding, people who, as the remainder of the chapter goes on to show, he can trust. It is to them, and to them alone, that he chooses to commit himself.

9

True or Temporary Believers?

Now when he was in Jerusalem at the passover, in the feast day, many believed in his name, when they saw the miracles which he did. But Jesus did not commit himself unto them, because he knew all men, And needed not that any should testify of man: for he knew what was in man.   John 2:23–25

We continue now with a consideration of what happened when our Lord went up to Jerusalem at the time of the Jewish Passover. We have already considered how he drove out those that sold oxen and sheep and doves, and the changers of money, and upset all their tables. And we have looked at what he said to them as he did so. We have also considered the reaction of the Jews – the Jewish leaders in particular.

Now here we have a comment from John the writer, the evangelist, on something further which happened during that visit to Jerusalem. And it is obvious that here John is continuing with the same theme and is making a further exposition of this whole question of signs.

Now, as we have been emphasising, the great concern of every Christian should be to make sure that he or she has received, and is receiving in ever increasing measure, of the blessed fullness, described in John 1:16: 'And of his fulness have all we received and grace for [upon] grace.' Obviously many difficulties arise with regard to that – there are problems – otherwise we all would be rejoicing in this fullness in all its abundance. There are clearly certain pitfalls, certain dangers. We must never forget the fact that we are confronted by an adversary, one who is not only our enemy but is still more the adversary of God and of our Lord Jesus Christ. The devil's greatest concern is that we should not receive of this fullness, his objective being, of course, to bring Christian salvation into disrepute and to mar and spoil the new creation as he did the first. So there are many things that we need to know and to learn, and, thank God, we are not left without instruction. So here we are given further instruction on this whole question of signs.

Now as we look at these verses, it is immediately quite clear that the people we are now looking at differ from the people we considered in the last study. There, we are confronted by Jewish leaders who are incapable of seeing the signs that our Lord has already given. They do not understand, for instance, what he was doing when he cleansed the Temple. They have missed the point completely. And that is why they ask him to do something spectacular.

But in the passage we are looking at now, we are

dealing with people who are in a very different category. Here are people who, when they saw the miracles or the signs, believed in his name. Now they want to follow him, they want to be his disciples. So here is a category which is different from the previous one and yet is still concerned about this whole matter of the signs.

There is, therefore, a problem confronting us and we must be aware of its character because what we find here is equally true today. The problem is as urgent now as when this incident took place. And the problem is that here we are looking at people who, though they are apparently doing the right things, are not accepted by our Lord. The difficulty with the others was that they did not appreciate the signs and therefore did not believe in him. But here are people who believe in his name because they have seen the signs. They seem to be the exact opposite of the previous group, and therefore we tend to think that they must of necessity be right, that these surely are the type of people our Lord will be anxious to have as his followers, people who can see the signs and understand them and accept them, and thereby wish to become his followers. But, we are told, 'Jesus did not commit himself unto them.' And therein lies the perplexity that faces us.

This is not unique, of course. We see the same thing in John 6:14–15 where we are told, 'Then those men, when they had seen the miracle that Jesus did, said, This is of a truth that prophet that should come into the world.' But then we read, 'When Jesus therefore perceived that they would come and take him by force, to make him a king, he departed again into a mountain himself alone.'

The same kind of person, the same kind of phenomenon.

There is also a statement of our Lord at the end of the Sermon on the Mount that seems to me to put the same problem very plainly:

> Not every one that saith unto me, Lord, Lord, shall enter into the kingdom of heaven; but he that doeth the will of my Father which is in heaven. Many will say to me in that day, Lord, Lord, have we not prophesied in thy name? and in thy name have cast out devils? and in thy name done many wonderful works? And then will I profess unto them, I never knew you: depart from me, ye that work iniquity.   Matthew 7:21–23

Here again are people who seem to glory in his signs. They call him 'Lord, Lord', and want to be his disciples and follow him because of what they have seen. Yet he repudiates them and says that he does not know them. He does not commit himself to them.

The essence of the problem is that at first sight our Lord's behaviour towards these people, his reaction to them, seems to be a contradiction of what is plainly and clearly his teaching elsewhere. I am referring to the teaching which is given in many places in which our Lord seems to argue that the people should have believed in him because of the signs. Take, for instance, John 10 where our Lord says to the Jews, 'If I do not the works of my Father, believe me not. But if I do, though ye believe not me, believe the works: that ye may know, and believe, that the Father is in me, and I in him' (verses 37–38). Then in John 12:37, we find,

'But though he had done so many miracles before them, yet they believed not on him.' Now that is obviously a condemnation of them: they should have believed.

There is another example in chapter 14:11 where our Lord says that his disciples should believe in him because of the works he has done: 'Believe me that I am in the Father, and the Father in me: or else believe me for the very works' sake' – a perfectly plain statement. And finally in chapter 15:24 we read: 'If I had not done among them the works which none other man did, they had not had sin: but now have they both seen and hated both me and my Father.'

Now the whole purport of all those statements is that the signs which he has worked render the people's unbelief inexcusable. It is as if the argument is: There are the signs, surely you must accept them and believe them. It is through them that you believe. Yet here, in chapter 2, we are dealing with people who claim to believe in him because of the signs. 'Many believed in his name, when they saw the miracles which he did.'

So how do we reconcile these things? It is clear that the signs should lead us to believe in him. That is why those who do not appreciate their significance are condemned. But it is made equally plain that belief in him and being impressed by the signs alone is not enough. And there we have the balance in this matter. The signs should lead us to believe in him, but if we only believe in him because of the signs we are in a defective position. One of the early Fathers of the church put this very well when he said, 'True faith is founded on God's word, not on wonders.'

What, then, are the principles underlying the teaching here? What was wrong with these people? First of all, we are told, '*Many* believed in his name when they saw the miracles which he did.' Here there is surely a preliminary lesson for us. Is this not the thing that preachers and evangelists today are out for – many believing! Great results! Surely we could expect our Lord to be delighted. He has come to gain followers, and here 'many believed in his name'. But he does not receive them.

This is a vital lesson for us. Surely in the light of this teaching we ought to consider again the whole question of pressing people to come to a decision. People are pressing upon him, and he pushes them back; he rejects them. Surely we must therefore be careful in this whole matter. We should be still more careful when we are animated by a desire for large numbers and great results. If you go through the Gospels carefully you will find that our Lord always sifted people in this way. That is a general warning for us arising out of these verses.

But as we look at what was wrong with these 'many' who believe in his name, we find the answer in this very phrase, 'believed in his name'. There is a great broad distinction between believing *in* his name, and believing *on* his name – believing in the name of the Lord Jesus and believing on the Lord Jesus Christ unto salvation.

And these people at the end of John 2 are a perfect illustration to us of those who do not believe truly. They think they do, but they do not. They believe in his name but have never believed on him. And that is why he does not commit himself unto them.

In the past, such people have sometimes been called

'temporary believers'. Another name has been 'false professors' – a designation favoured by the Puritans in particular. A good deal has been written in the New Testament about these false professors of the Christian faith. It seems to me that the five foolish virgins in our Lord's parable of the ten virgins are typical. The ten virgins can be divided into two groups – five foolish, five wise. Though their general appearance is similar, though in a sense they are all disciples, they are not in the same position. There is a fundamental and vital difference between the two groups, and it becomes an eternal difference because at the critical moment the door is shut in the face of the foolish virgins. So this is a most solemn and serious matter.

It is exactly the same thing, surely, in the case of the people we read about at the beginning of the sixth chapter of Hebrews. Here are people who have made a profession of faith and have had certain great experiences; they have 'tasted of the heavenly gift . . . and the powers of the world to come' (verses 4–5). Yet it is perfectly clear that they were never regenerate. They were never truly Christian at all.

Again, John, in his first epistle, describes exactly the same type of people. Dealing with the question of the Antichrist, he says, 'Little children, it is the last time: and as ye have heard that anti-christ shall come, even now are there many anti-christs; whereby we know that it is the last time.' Then he continues: 'They went out from us, but they were not of us; for if they had been of us, they would no doubt have continued with us: but they went out, that they might be made manifest that they were not all of us' (1 John 2:18–19). Now these people had belonged to the church, they had appeared to be of the true body of disciples. They were people who had said, 'Yes, we believe,' and had been received into the church. But after a while they had gone out. And they had done that, says John, because they were 'not of us': 'for if they had been of us, they would no doubt have continued with us'. They were temporary believers. They had a false belief which at first gave the impression of being a true belief. Even the apostles, the leaders of the church, could not recognise them for what they were. But here in John 2 we are told that our Lord knows exactly; he recognises them at once.

So how do we recognise these people? What are the characteristics of these 'temporary believers', this wrong belief, this thing that appears so right on the surface but which our Lord will not accept? Now it is quite clear, is it not, that these people are attracted to the gospel, they are interested. To use the modern term, they are intrigued by him. They are anxious to be his followers. They seem to be true converts. They want to be accepted into the community.

What is the attraction? Well, it is obvious that they are attracted by the Lord himself, by his person. And that is as true today as it was then. Here are people who are interested in our Lord. Why? It is because he is unique. He is a kind of spectacle, a kind of phenomenon. Just consider the position: here are people who are accustomed to the Pharisees and their teaching, and to the teaching of the Sadducees. To be a scribe or a teacher of the law a man has to undergo considerable training and preparation. So the people listen to their religious leaders as the compare and contrast what the authorities have said on thousands of detailed questions. The teachers and scribes are men of vast erudition and learning, and they speak on the basis of this knowledge.

But here, suddenly, there comes this extraordinary person, a carpenter from, of all places, a northern village called Nazareth. 'Can any good thing come out of Nazareth?' (John 1:46) is a proverbial saying. But here, without any of this training or preparation, he suddenly appears before them; something absolutely new.

Now there are people who are always attracted by the novel. They are like the people of Athens to whom Paul spoke and of whom we are told they 'spent their time in nothing else, but either to tell, or to hear some new thing' (Acts 17:21). We are familiar with that kind of attitude. Here is a new phenomenon, here is a new teacher, and especially one who teaches with authority. He does not just compare and quote authorities but stands up and says, 'I say to you.'

And there are people who, when they hear a word or a note of authority like that, are always ready to listen and believe. There is a craving for authority. It no doubt accounts in a large measure for the return of people to the Church of Rome. Many who have done so have said in their autobiographies that that was the reason. Any kind of movement that appears to speak with authority will always attract certain types of persons.

But then these people at the end of John chapter 2 also like our Lord's teaching. Here is a critic of Judaism, a critic of the old religious tradition. He has just proved it by turning those people out of the Temple.

There is the old religion and all its paraphernalia, and he is a revolutionary. Now that in and of itself always makes a very great appeal to some people. They like to feel that they have made a discovery of something of which the church through all the centuries has been completely ignorant. So they are attracted by anything that has a novel note, that seems to come from an entirely different angle and propose something that has never been known before.

But then still more, of course, is the fact of the miracles, the signs themselves. Here again is something which is dealt with in many places in the New Testament. There is the story of Simon the sorcerer, Simon Magus – a typical illustration of this interest in the phenomenal (Acts 8:9–24). I have already touched on people's desire for signs, but let me put it on a different level. This is the kind of thing that is often seen during a period of revival and religious awakening. There has never yet been a revival but that with the revival tide many people have been washed up on to the shore who have never become true believers and do not belong to the church. The tidal movement of the Spirit seems to take them up and to carry them along. If there is a mass evangelistic campaign and they see others going forward, instinctively they also get up and go forward. They say everything that is right, and seem to be truly Christian, but subsequent events show that they were never truly Christian at all. Now I am not suggesting that they are dishonest. They are not. That is not the difficulty. But they are unwittingly deceiving themselves. They are merely moved by the religious excitement which is the result of something unusual happening.

The vital distinction that surely comes out in this whole episode is the difference between credulity and true faith. Credulity is the mentality which is ready to believe anything whatsoever. It is open to anything new or interesting or exciting, and becomes a victim to it. And it will do this many, many times, even taking up teachings which are entirely contradictory. Credulous people fall for the last thing they have heard.

Most of us are, up to a point, subject to credulity. On the other hand, some people are so afraid of this that they are not open to anything. They are hardened against everything and they quench the Spirit. They remain in their self-invented security, and have never known any touch of the Holy Spirit of God. That is not the true antithesis of credulity. The true antithesis is a living and a real and a sound faith. We must examine ourselves to make very sure of these matters.

The spirit of credulity is general and may be something which we are born with, but we must realise what we are born with. We all have something particular to fight. We must get to know ourselves and our own dangers, and we must always be unusually careful with regard to them.

However, in addition to credulity, there is something further, and that is that a wrong motive tends to creep in, especially when phenomena are apparent. That is the great warning in the case of Simon Magus. Everything we are told about that man points in that direction. Let me single out some verses in particular from Acts 8: 'Then Simon himself believed also: and when he was baptized, he continued with Philip, and wondered, beholding the miracles and signs which were done' (verse 13). You see, already we are given an insight. This is what was captivating him. We are not told that he was increasingly amazed at the teaching, at the doctrine, that Philip was propounding. No, no, he was excited by the miracles and signs.

Then we read: 'And when Simon saw that through the laying on of the apostles' hands the Holy Ghost was given, he offered them money, saying, Give me also this power, that on whomsoever I lay hands, he may receive the Holy Ghost' (verses 18–19). This is the desire to be important, the desire to be prominent, the desire to be a possessor of gifts that enable you to do things.

Again, this appeals to the natural man or woman, especially in certain types of people. But we are all to some extent guilty. We all like to be prominent, we all like notoriety, we all like praise, we all like to be important. It is innate in humanity as the result of sin and the Fall. Now that desire can creep in even into the spiritual realm. We see things happening and we say, 'Ah, if only I could do that, how wonderful it would be!' Oh, let us all examine ourselves, my dear friends! Let us beware of the desire to be a great preacher, the desire to be a great anything; the devil is always there. You may have heard the story about John Bunyan who had just preached and was leaving, when somebody came and praised him and said, 'What a wonderful sermon!' But John Bunyan understood these matters and said, 'It's all right, the devil has already told me that!'

Now if you were a preacher you would not laugh at that, you would weep! That was the spirit in Simon Magus. Here it is, this terrible spirit, this desire that says, 'I would like to be doing this, I would like to have this, so that I can talk about it and people will be talking about me.' Furthermore, the element of merchandise comes in, and here James has a striking and salutary warning: 'Ye lust, and have not: ye kill, and desire to have, and cannot obtain: ye fight and war, yet ye have not, because ye ask not. Ye ask, and receive not' – why? – 'because ye ask amiss, that ye may consume it upon your lusts' (James 4:2–3). Now 'lusts' there does not mean fleshly sex but lust for power, lust for notoriety, lust for prominence, lust for greatness, lust for authority.

These are terrible things, and our Lord, who knows everything, knows why people profess to believe in him when they see the signs. He knows when they are animated by something base, something unworthy and mercenary, which panders only to the flesh. And there is no doubt but that this was the position of a large number of people in the church at Corinth, and that is why Paul ever had to write the twelfth, thirteenth and fourteenth chapters of 1 Corinthians. The believers who lived in Corinth were boasting and vying with one another concerning the gifts. They were giving prominence to tongues in a way that they should not. Paul had to rebuke them because they had lost their balance and were despising and envying one another. Now when you get into that sort of state, you are interested in gifts in an entirely wrong sense. You want something from God in order to 'consume it upon your lusts' in some way (James 4:3).

There were people in the church at Corinth (let us be fair) who were doing exactly the same thing with their great intellectual understanding. They are the people dealt with in the eighth chapter and Paul says to them:

'Knowledge puffeth up, but charity edifieth' (verse 1). It can happen in any realm, not only with the more spectacular gifts but with the study of doctrine, and knowledge of the Bible. Oh, you can boast of your understanding of theology, you can feel proud of yourself. But your real reason for studying and reading is to show off your great knowledge.

Those, then, are the general characteristics of these people, and human nature does not change. There are people today who think they are truly Christian but all they have is a general interest in 'Jesus' as they generally call him. Not 'the Lord Jesus Christ' but 'Jesus'. They are interested in Jesus and in his teaching. They write books about him. They talk to one another about him. They are interested in the Bible. I have known people who have had, it seems to me, nothing but a purely technical interest in the Bible. They are clever at turning up this and that verse and comparing them. They have topics and words all neatly classified. In a minute they can give you an analysis of a whole book of the Bible. But that is not true knowledge of the Scripture! And, as we have seen, they are interested in phenomena and signs.

So what is the real trouble with these people? It is that their position is not based on the word. It is not based on biblical teaching. That is the fundamental trouble. And because of that, of course, it is superficial. In other words, the real trouble with such people is that their belief in his name is always partial. Their response to him is incomplete.

There are some people who believe in the name of the Lord Jesus Christ with their heads only. They have a theoretical knowledge, an intellectual belief, or a philosophical approach to him, but their hearts have never been touched, they have never been moved, they have never been melted. And their wills have not been touched. All this great knowledge has never changed their lives. It does not govern their conduct and behaviour. They live like worldly people, which is what they are. Worldly people can take an intellectual interest in the teaching of the Christian faith. I have often said that it is such a glorious system, looked at as a system of truth, that any intelligent man or woman ought to be attracted by it, and many such people have been attracted. But it has only been intellectual, it has never gone any further. That is one kind of defective, false profession.

Then in the case of other people, only the heart is touched. They have sometimes even been encouraged in this. They have heard preachers saying, 'Stop thinking, let yourselves go.' And they have let themselves go. Their minds have not been in operation at all. They have deliberately abandoned the intellect. They have allowed their feelings to be disturbed – a riot of the feelings and of the imagination – but there is no understanding. In fact, they may have been told, 'It does not matter whether you understand or not, the great thing is that you are getting this experience.' The understanding is not involved and, alas, so often with such people the will is also never engaged.

Then there is a third group in which Christianity is almost entirely a matter of the will. They do not trouble to understand, and they are not interested in their feelings. They have been told, 'If thou shalt confess with

thy mouth . . . thou shalt be saved' (Romans 10:9).
They have been told they must *do* something, and they
are always ready to do things. They are not interested in
intellectual comprehension, and they know that the
heart can be very deceitful. So they say, 'What I like is a
message which tells me that all that is necessary is to start
doing something.' And that is all they have – activity.

But one of the fundamental points about this message,
this gospel, is that it takes up the entire person. 'But
God be thanked,' wrote Paul, 'that ye were the servants
of sin, but ye have obeyed from the heart that form of
doctrine which was delivered you' (Romans 6:17). And
if the whole of you is not engaged, you can be certain
you are a false professor.

There, then, are the characteristics of the people who
have only believed in his name. Such people have never
believed on him, they have never truly committed
themselves to him. In the original Greek the same word
is used for 'believed' in verse 23 and 'commit' in verse
24. 'Many *believed* in his name when they saw the miracles that he did, but Jesus did not *commit himself unto
them*' – or 'did not *believe in them*'. So these people
have never committed themselves to him. Theirs has
only been the superficial kind of belief that I have been
illustrating.

The trouble is that these people have completely mis-
understood him. And you will find many examples of
that as you go through the Gospels. They think they
have understood him, but they have not. Here are
people who are interested in him as a miracle worker.
You remember the people in John 6, who tried to 'take
him by force, to make him a king' (verse 15). They

were interested in him as king. Others were interested in him as a political agitator; others as a healer.

And all these types are still about. They regard themselves as Christians. But they pick out only what appeals to them, and, because of that, and because he has done the thing they wanted, they believe in him. You can easily think through these various categories for yourself. They have never really seen him as he is, but are interested in different aspects of his activity. So their belief is partial both with regard to themselves and with regard to him.

Perhaps the best way of showing you this is to show you the great contrast between these people and people like Andrew and Philip of whom we read in the first chapter of John. This is the true reaction. Andrew, you remember, has been with him, and then we are told, 'He first findeth his own brother Simon, and saith unto him . . .' – what? 'We have found a miracle worker. We have found one who does signs. We have found one who is going to be the king'? No, he says, 'We have found the Messias, which is, being interpreted, the Christ' (John 1:41). You see the depth? Andrew has an insight into who our Lord is, and why he has come.

It is exactly the same in the case of Philip: 'Philip findeth Nathanael, and saith unto him, We have found him, of whom Moses in the law, and the prophets, did write, Jesus of Nazareth, the son of Joseph' (John 1:45). Philip is interested in the person, in the totality of the person. He has a glimpse into the ultimate. He is not concerned about partial things or exciting, immediate things.

And the same is true with Nathanael himself.

'Nathanael answereth and saith unto him, Rabbi, thou art the Son of God; thou art the King of Israel' (verse 49). Now what makes him say that? It is because our Lord has said to him, 'Before that Philip called thee, when thou wast under the fig tree, I saw thee' (verse 48). But Nathanael does not turn to him and say, 'You are wonderful, because you seem to be able to see even through the leaves and everything. You have some extraordinary psychic power. I'm tremendously interested and intrigued by this kind of phenomenon.' Not at all! 'Rabbi, thou art the Son of God' – not a miracle worker, not this partial understanding.

But these people at Jerusalem have never seen that. They have never seen him in the glory of his person. They have no understanding at all of him as Saviour. They do not realise why he has come into the world. They think he has come to perform these phenomena. But he has not. The phenomena are to lead to him, to an understanding of who he is, and if you stop with the phenomena he will not commit himself to you. These people think they are going after him for the right reason, they are praising him and they want to be his disciples, but he does not commit himself to them.

But, finally, the real trouble with these people is that they have never seen themselves properly. They have never seen themselves as helpless, hopeless sinners. Oh, they have felt the need for a bit of help, and a bit of advice, and a bit of teaching, and a good example, and they go to 'Jesus' for these things. But that is all. They are not completely helpless. How unlike Peter they are!

One night, Peter and the others go out fishing and catch nothing. Then our Lord comes to them and says:

Go out again and throw the net on the other side. And they catch so many that the net breaks. An amazing miracle! But Peter does not say, 'Let me follow you, marvellous miracle worker that you are.' No, we read this: 'He fell down at Jesus' knees, saying, Depart from me; for I am a sinful man, O Lord' (Luke 5:4–11). One of the best signs of true believers is they are always men and women who have been humbled.

These people have never been humbled – never. They are still in charge of themselves, and, being in charge of themselves, they decide to join us. 'Ah,' they say, 'this is what we want. This is the kind of teacher we're going to follow.' And standing up, full of confidence, they decide to join him. They are too healthy. They have never been convicted. They have never been cast to the ground. They have never cried out, 'Men and brethren, what shall we do?' (Acts 2:37). They 'decide for Christ'. And they have been seen in meetings before now talking to one another saying, 'Shall we go forward or shall we not?' They have even been known to pat their hair tidy before they decide to go forward! That is health, not brokenness. That is not humility. That is not being convicted by the Holy Spirit.

True believers are those who have seen the blessed person and seen themselves, and say, 'Depart from me; for I am a sinful man, O Lord.' True believers are men and women who have heard him say something like this: 'Whosoever will come after me, let him deny himself' – no self-interest, no self-trust or self-confidence – 'let him deny himself, and take up his cross, and follow me' (Mark 8:34). Not a life of miraculous excitement and thrills. No, no! There is a cross-bearing element in

it. You deliberately take up your cross and follow him
withersoever he may lead. You are not in charge. You
do not decide what you want. You do not pick and
choose. You do not eye things like a Simon Magus. No,
no! But the other people have been summed up once
and for ever in this phrase: 'This people honoureth me
with their lips; but their heart is far from me' (Matthew
15:8).

May God give us grace to examine ourselves. We
claim to be his followers, do we not? But what is
our interest in him? What is our view of him? What
is our ultimate desire?

Has he committed himself to us? That is the question. How do we know that? We can examine ourselves. I have already given some tests. We can examine
ourselves in the light of these people and of similar
people who have been put before us in the different
parts of the Scripture. Let us realise the terrible possibility that he may look upon us and say, 'I never knew
you: depart from me, ye that work iniquity' (Matthew
7:23).

10

A Personal Relationship

Now when he was in Jerusalem at the passover, in the feast day, many believed in his name, when they saw the miracles which he did. But Jesus did not commit himself unto them, because he knew all men, And needed not that any should testify of man: for he knew what was in man.   John 2:23–25

We come back to a further study of this incident recorded here at the end of this second chapter of John's Gospel. We have seen that our Lord will never commit himself to those who are healthy, to those who come standing on their own feet, as it were, saying they are interested in him and propose to follow him. He will not commit himself to them. He said, 'I am not come to call the righteous, but sinners to repentance' (Matthew 9:13). 'They that be whole need not a physician, but they that are sick' (Matthew 9:12). He will not receive people who are just interested in him in general, or interested in Christianity in general. He will have nothing to do with such people. And that is the lesson that we have learned so far.

But we cannot leave it at that because that, in a sense, leaves out the most important aspect of this particular incident. So far we have been looking at it only from the standpoint of our attitude, and what we do and think and say. But the really important thing which is taught here is his attitude and what he does and says. And let me again remind you that what we have fundamentally in our minds is the great controlling thought of the whole of this Gospel according to St John. We are concerned about receiving that life which partakes of his fullness, and grace upon grace. That is what we are meant for, that is essential Christianity.

But we are confronted by a powerful and subtle enemy, who will do everything he can to prevent our receiving of that fullness and attaining that kind of life. And, thank God, we are therefore given teaching. We are shown some of the dangers and pitfalls that stand in our way. And I suggest that this is one of them and a very important one: though they appear to believe in him, he will not commit himself to them.

What, then, is the further teaching with regard to this? I have tried to extract the principles and will put them to you in the form of a number of propositions. The first – and in many ways the most important thing we can ever learn – is that salvation, after all, is a personal relationship with the Lord Jesus Christ himself. The whole incident here focuses our attention upon the relationship of these people to him – what they did and what he did.

I put it like that because one of the greatest dangers

for all of us, and particularly, perhaps, for those who believe in the importance of doctrine, of theology and divine truth, as every Christian should, is to forget that salvation is a matter of that personal relationship and to look upon it merely as the acceptance of a creed and holding to correct teaching. This is a real danger. We see it not only in the Scriptures but in the long history of the Christian church. The danger is always to move from a vital living relationship to him to a dead orthodoxy.

Now orthodoxy is absolutely essential, but if we substitute belief in, and the acceptance of, a number of doctrines for a living relationship with him, we have lost everything. What makes us Christian is not that we believe the right things. You cannot, of course, be a Christian without that, but a mere belief in the right things does not constitute salvation because the essence of salvation is this personal relationship – 'He did not commit himself unto them.' People who do not have this relationship have nothing, though they may have a kind of belief on the basis of our Lord's miracles and signs.

A second and constant danger that comes when we think of salvation in an impersonal manner, is to think of it as if it were money in a bank, or a liquid contained in a tank from which we can draw. We behave as if there is a great deposit of grace, a store, a reserve, of salvation, and we go in and we draw from that. We regard the blessings as a kind of force or power, or an influence. But if we merely look at it like that, we are violating the great principle that salvation is not something material but is always a personal relationship between believers and their Lord.

A third danger – and there is nothing more fatal – is the danger of thinking of salvation as something which is one-sided, with the activity entirely on our side. This follows from the previous points. If there is a great store of salvation, then of course the vital question is: How often do we go and draw from that, like the woman of Samaria going back and forth to the well to draw this water? There are many who seem to think of salvation entirely like that, so the whole emphasis is upon their activity. It all depends upon what they do. Are they 'abiding'? Are they taking? But here, at the very beginning of John's Gospel, is given the lie direct. The essence of salvation is that it is a two-sided personal relationship: he and the believer.

Then the second proposition, which follows by a logical necessity from the first, is also clearly seen in this incident. We cannot decide to take salvation or any part of it whenever we like. This is a most urgent principle. Here are people who, having seen the miracles, believe in him and approach him. But he does not commit himself unto them. They have decided for him but that decision does not save them.

All teaching which says that *we* can decide for Christ is automatically false. We must never represent salvation in that way. Sometimes we are told, 'You have the power of decision. You have your free will. In every person there is an element of faith. Whenever you travel by train you have faith in the engine driver, otherwise you would never enter that train at all. Faith,' we are told, 'is a natural quality, and all you must do is listen to what we are telling you, then exercise this free will and faith which you have as a human being and decide to "go in for it". And you can do it now, there is nothing to stop you. Why do you hesitate?'

Can anyone still go on saying that after looking at this incident? 'Many believed in his name, when they saw the miracles which he did. But Jesus did not commit himself unto them.' We do not determine this matter, and it is wrong to put the emphasis upon our decision. There is a sense in which we cannot decide for Christ. I know that the man or woman who has heard the gospel, and truly believes, is all out to make a decision, but we must never speak or preach as if salvation depended entirely upon our point of view, our activity or our decision.

This point is not only vital in evangelism but in every part and in every stage of the Christian life. There is a teaching with regard to sanctification and to the baptism of the Holy Spirit – they are not the same; I am referring to two separate things – there is a teaching with regard to both these aspects of the Christian experience which tells us that we can have them whenever we like. All we must do, we are told, is 'take it by faith'. We are told, 'Do you believe this teaching? Very well, if you do, take God at his word. Ask him for it and thank him that you have it.' They say, 'Don't worry about your feelings. You may feel nothing at all. It doesn't matter, take it by faith.'

Now I am suggesting that that is of necessity a wrong teaching. There is no 'it' that you can take. There is nothing material, no mass of substance. As we have just seen, we are not talking about a volume of liquid that you can draw from. It is always personal.

And because of that you cannot 'take it by faith'. You cannot take the baptism of the Spirit by faith. You cannot take sanctification by faith. It is a sheer impossibility because of this fundamental personal relationship.

And, of course, on many other grounds we could also show you why this view is essentially false. I have sometimes put it like this – I know a number of people who have taken so much by faith that they have nothing! They have had no experience at all; they are just 'taking it by faith'. If you examine yourselves in the light of your experience, and especially in the light of the experience of the saints of the centuries, you cannot believe in this teaching of 'taking it by faith'. We talked about this in an earlier study. When people are baptised with the Spirit, they know it. It is something experiential. Furthermore, sanctification is not something you can take in one act. It grows, and you can test yourself to see whether or not it is going on progressively. Moreover, we are concerned now with these fundamental, primary principles. These people thought that they could go and take salvation. But they could not.

The third proposition, the vital matter in connection with this whole subject, is whether he commits himself to us and believes in us. We are entirely dependent upon him and his attitude towards us. These people, in a sense, did everything they could but it availed them nothing. You can bombard the door, but he alone can open it. Ample confirmation of this teaching runs right through the whole of the Scripture, but the parable of the ten virgins alone settles this.

I have already emphasised that we must have the right attitude to him and to our need, but even that does not save us. We are saved by what he does. Our salvation is entirely his prerogative. It is entirely in his hands and he does not commit himself to all who approach him.

In this whole matter of salvation and all the blessings of salvation, there is, as we have seen, a secret element, and people are often perplexed by this. It is a fact that the professors of Christianity can be divided into two groups: those who are true and those who are false. Ten virgins – five wise, five foolish. On the surface there is scarcely any difference, like the two houses, one built on the rock, one on the sand. The difference in those houses is in the foundation – the hidden element. He commits himself to some, he does not commit himself to others. How do you know? Well, there is only one answer to that:

> The love of Jesus what it is,
> None but His loved ones know.
> *Latin, 12th century*
> *Translated by Edward Caswell*

They know; nobody else does.

We have already looked at this subject of secrecy, and I do not want to stay with it now, but there is wonderful teaching with regard to it in the New Testament. Take, for instance, the statement of the apostle Paul: 'He that is spiritual judgeth' – he understands, he knows – 'all things, yet he himself is judged of no man' (1 Corinthians 2:15). Paul has been saying that 'the natural man receiveth not the things of the Spirit of God: for they are foolishness unto him: neither can he know them, because they are spiritually discerned'. In other words, the spiritual person has a secret. He has been given understanding by the Spirit, and the other man does not understand him now. They were once exactly the same – two natural men with the same lack of understanding. But one has received the mystic secret: 'God hath revealed them unto us by his Spirit: for the Spirit searcheth all things, yea, the deep things of God' (1 Corinthians 2:10). So here is a man who has understanding, while the other man has not, though he may want it and may be striving for it. Many people 'make their decisions' and go forward in meetings but that does not mean that they will all receive the blessing or that they are all Christians. *He* decides. 'Jesus did not commit himself unto them.'

That, then, brings me to the practical question: How may we know whether or not he has committed himself to us? We are interested in him and interested in his kingdom, interested in what he teaches and in what he does. But the question is: Are we Christians? We have made the effort, and we are considering these things, yes; but these people go forward to him at Jerusalem saying they have believed in him and want to join the company, and they are refused. So the question is: Has he committed himself to us? And again the answer is:

> The love of Jesus what it is
> None but His loved ones know.

They know. 'He that is spiritual judgeth all things, yet he himself is judged of no man.'

Now how is this to be interpreted? Notice that here

in Jerusalem our Lord's refusal is obvious. He makes it plain to them that he does not receive them. He does not say to them, 'Follow me; join the company. Come among us and I will lead you on.' How different to the treatment given to a man like Nathanael. Nathanael has been brought to him, and has believed in him. And when he makes his great confession: 'Rabbi, thou art the Son of God; thou art the King of Israel,' Jesus answers, 'Because I said unto thee, I saw thee under the fig tree, believest thou?' – then – 'thou shalt see greater things than these' (John 1:49–51). Now that is the very thing he does not say to these other people. He receives Nathanael: '[Jesus] saith unto him, Verily, verily I say unto you, Hereafter ye shall see heaven open, and the angels of God ascending and descending upon the Son of man' (verse 51). He does not say that to these people at the feast in Jerusalem. That is exactly the difference. He makes it obvious that they are not going to be led into the secrets. They are not to be given further instruction. They have come so far in their own energy, but it is all of the flesh, and he does not receive them.

As we continue to read the story of our Lord's ministry, we find that he continues very much in the same way. He draws a distinction among the people who listen to him and who seem to be responding to his message. He has secret things to say to the believers, those to whom he commits himself, but not to the others. There is a very good instance of this just at the end of the healing of that poor boy at the foot of the Mount of Transfiguration.

Our Lord has gone up to the Mount with Peter and James and John, and he has been transfigured before them. But as they come down from the mountain they see a great multitude around the rest of the apostles and disciples, and 'the scribes questioning with them'. Then we are told, 'And straightway all the people, when they beheld him, were greatly amazed, and running to him saluted him. And he asked the scribes, What question ye with them?' (Matthew 9:14–16). And then the story comes out. A man says that he has brought his son to the disciples asking them to deliver the boy from the dumb spirit that is tormenting him, but they have completely failed. And then, after a discussion between the father and our Lord, our Lord drives the evil spirit out of this boy and restores him to his father, perfectly whole.

Then we read this in verses 28 and 29: 'And when he was come into the house' – they have left the crowd now – 'his disciples asked him *privately* . . .' Oh, here is the whole thing! Have you got this private access to him? The people at the feast in Jerusalem never ask him anything privately. They are not allowed to be with him privately. He does not receive them. He does not commit himself to them. But the disciples are allowed to ask him privately, 'Why could not we cast him out?' And our Lord says, 'This kind can come forth by nothing, but by prayer and fasting.'

There is another illustration of the same thing in Matthew 13. Our Lord has just finished telling the parable of the sower, and we read, 'The disciples came, and said unto him, Why speakest thou unto them in parables? He answered and said unto them' – here is the distinction – 'because it is given unto *you* to know the mysteries of the kingdom of heaven, but to them it is not given. For whosoever hath, to him shall be given, and he shall have more abundance: but whosoever hath not, from him shall be taken away even that he hath' (Matthew 13:10–12).

Now at first the Pharisees and scribes and everybody else all came and listened together and an observer could not tell any difference. But our Lord knew the difference the whole time. He deliberately gave much of his teaching in the form of parables in order that the Pharisees and scribes might not understand. He says, 'Therefore speak I to them in parables: because they seeing see not; and hearing they hear not, neither do they understand' – and they are not allowed to understand. He quotes Isaiah: 'This people's heart is waxed gross, and their ears are dull of hearing, and their eyes they have closed; lest at any time they should see with their eyes, and hear with their ears, and should understand with their heart, and should be converted, and I should heal them. But blessed are your eyes, for they see: and your ears, for they hear' (Matthew 13:13–16). Here is this fundamental distinction. He does not commit himself to Pharisees and scribes, but he does commit himself to the disciples, and to humble, true believers.

That, then, is how our Lord revealed himself to his followers in the days of his flesh, but we also have another very interesting illustration after his return to glory. Saul of Tarsus was famous as a violent persecutor of the church. We are told, 'He made havock of the church' (Acts 8:3); 'breathing out threatenings and slaughter' (Acts 9:1). Yet a great encounter with our Lord takes place on the road to Damascus, and Saul cries out from the ground, 'Lord, what wilt thou have me to do?' (Acts 9:6). And Jesus commits himself unto Saul. He trusts him. He tells him what is going to happen. To me, what is so wonderful in that story is that our Lord not only lets Saul of Tarsus know at once that he has received him and is trusting him, he lets other people know it also. Ananias is very afraid when he receives the commandment to go and baptise Paul, but he is told to go and do it: 'He [Paul] is a chosen vessel unto me' (Acts 9:15), says the risen Lord.

Our Lord reassures Barnabas and through Barnabas he reassures the other disciples at Jerusalem. They are all afraid of this man, because they have heard such terrible things about him. But the Lord himself guarantees him. He says: I trust this man. I am going to use him. He will be a minister and a witness. 'He is a chosen vessel unto me' (Acts 9:15). You trust him, because I trust him.

Jesus *committed* himself unto Saul, while the people were afraid to do so. He generally reverses all our decisions. He receives 'publicans and sinners' and rejects Pharisees and scribes. The church of God is a most surprising place, and I think that at the final judgement we shall be yet more astonished at the things we shall see and discover.

So there it is in the Scriptures, in the days of our Lord's flesh and immediately after his ascension, but how does he commit himself to us now? Thank God, we are not left in ignorance. The Scriptures give us abundant satisfaction in answer to our question. Can we know whether he has committed himself to us? Thank God, we can. How do we know it? Well, it is, as I say, the whole question of our relationship to him. That is the only thing that matters. And it is as we assess that, that we know exactly where we are.

Let me, then, give you just a few negatives to start with. Who are the people whom he does not receive? They are the people who rest on their decision. If you are resting on your decision for Christ, I suggest to you that he has not received you, he has not committed himself to you. It follows inevitably. The people to whom he commits himself are resting on what he does, not on what they themselves do. So those who say, 'I have decided for Christ,' are those to whom you should put your questions.

Then there are the people who always have to reassure themselves that they are Christians, who are troubled constantly about it, those who have to 'prove' to themselves that they are. At the very least such people are in a very doubtful position. And the people who always have to go back to something that they once did are in the same miserable state. These people are always having to look back at the decision they once took or at some wonderful experience they once had. For them, it is not always the Lord immediately, directly, in the present but a past experience. A man gets up and says with a good deal of braggadocio, 'It is now twenty years since I decided for Christ and I have never regretted it.' Oh, what a terrible thing to say! In the light of this great and wonderful teaching, his position is very dubious.

So now we must examine ourselves. Are you resting on any of those things? Are you resting on your decision? Are you resting upon some experience that you had a long time ago? Are you having to prove to yourself constantly that you are a Christian?

However, let us leave the negatives and come to the positives: How do men and women know whether or not Christ has committed himself to them? First, they are the people who are surprised at themselves. I say this on the authority of one of the greatest Christians, perhaps the greatest Christian, that the church has ever known, the mighty apostle Paul. Listen to how he speaks about himself. He never talks about his 'decision for Christ', but says:

> And I thank Christ Jesus our Lord, who hath enabled me, for that he counted me faithful, putting me into the ministry; who was before a blasphemer, and a persecutor, and injurious: but I obtained mercy, because I did it ignorantly in unbelief. And the grace of our Lord was exceeding abundant with faith and love which is in Christ Jesus. This is a faithful saying, and worthy of all acceptation, that Christ Jesus came into the world to save sinners; of whom I am chief. Howbeit for this cause I obtained mercy, that in me first Jesus Christ might shew forth all longsuffering, for a pattern to them which should hereafter believe on him to life everlasting.
>
> 1 Timothy 1:12–16

Paul was amazed at himself; he never got over it. He says to the Galatians, '. . . I live; yet not I, but Christ liveth in me . . . the Son of God, who loved me, and gave himself for me' (Galatians 2:20). 'For I am the least of the apostles, that am not meet to be called an apostle . . .' (1 Corinthians 15:9). Here it is, a sense of unworthiness, a sense of uncleanness, a sense of amazement that one is in this Christian life at all:

> And can it be, that I should gain
>   An interest in the Saviour's blood?
> Died He for me, who caused His pain;
>   For me, who Him to death pursued?
> Amazing love! how can it be
> That Thou, my God, shouldst die for me?
>
> *Charles Wesley*

People who feel that, are those to whom he has committed himself beyond any doubt. They have nothing in themselves, and they are amazed at the fact that they are in the Christian life at all and are counted among the redeemed.

And, of course, what follows from that is a deep sense of gratitude. 'I thank Christ Jesus, my Lord, who hath enabled me, for that he counted me faithful.' How could Paul do it? I cannot trust myself – 'In me (that is, in my flesh,) dwelleth no good thing' (Romans 8:18). But God has done it all because of his grace and his love and his compassion. Those who know this are filled with a sense of gratitude to him, and when they give their testimony, they do not talk about themselves nor about what they did, but about what Christ has done to them, and they pour out their praise and gratitude and thanksgiving to him.

And then another thing is this: people to whom our Lord commits himself – and again they are amazed at this – find that they have a certain amount of spiritual understanding. They are no longer interested just in stories, testimonies, or in accounts of marvellous things but in spiritual truth. The great chapter on that is 1 Corinthians 2. The apostle points out how the princes of this world did not recognise our Lord when he was here in the flesh: 'For had they known it,' he says, 'they would not have crucified the Lord of glory.' But then, drawing a great contrast, Paul continues, 'But as it is written, Eye hath not seen, nor ear heard, neither have entered into the heart of man, the things which God hath prepared for them that love him' – these secret things that he has prepared – 'But God hath revealed them unto us by his Spirit' (1 Corinthians 2:8–10). And we know that because Paul says again in verse 12, 'We have received, not the spirit of the world, but the spirit which is of God; that we might know the things that are freely given to us of God.' And then the most amazing thing comes in the last verse of chapter 2: 'Who hath known the mind of the Lord, that he may instruct him?' And the answer: 'We have the mind of Christ' (verse 16). If you find you have an element of spiritual understanding, you can be quite certain that he has committed himself to you. You have been 'born again', you have a seed of eternal life.

I am not talking about a mechanical knowledge of the Bible. I am talking now about an insight and an understanding of spiritual truth, spiritual realities; you think in a spiritual manner. And you are interested in that – not so much in the application of Christianity to this and that issue, but in this inner understanding. You feel you are inside the Bible and looking round you, not always looking objectively from the outside.

Spiritual perception and understanding! If you have any of that in you, he has received you.

And then, of course, it follows from all this that you have a sense of rest and of peace. You no longer say, 'O when shall all my striving cease!' This is something that one cannot put into words, but there is a rest of the soul and he alone can give it. He has his ways of intimating to us that he has committed himself to us. And I would say that this element of rest and of peace and of quiet is always essential in true faith. You are no longer seeking, searching. You know that he has met with you. There is a fundamental rest. That does not mean you are perfect, it does not mean you are satisfied – of course not. But it does mean that the foundation is certain. It is clear. You are not troubled about that. You are no longer having to prove to yourself that you are a Christian. There are many uncertain things still, but *that* is settled once and for ever.

What else? Well, here is another point and to me it is one of the most important of all. It is a sense you have that you have been dealt with. We started off by saying that salvation is ultimately a matter of personal relationship with him, and in a personal relationship there is, of course, activity on the two sides. But when it is a relationship with the Lord of glory, the relationship is mainly on his side. And so you become conscious that you are being dealt with, that your life is in the hands of another. 'Oh,' says Paul, 'For as many as are led by the Spirit of God, they are the sons of God' (Romans 8:14). 'Work out your own salvation with fear and trembling. For it is God which worketh in you both to will and to do . . .' (Philippians 2:12–13).

You are conscious that he is working in you. It is difficult to put it into words, but in the whole of your life you are most deeply aware that you are no longer your own, that you belong to another, to One who is leading and directing you, and continually interferes in your life.

Let me put it then like this: the element of surprise is again in your life, not the original surprise, but surprise in the sense that he surprises us. I have already quoted this hymn – it puts this very well:

> Sometimes a light surprises
> The Christian while he sings.
> *William Cowper*

You are having a hard time, the clouds have gathered over you, and everything is stagnant and stale. You are unhappy and you do not understand it. You feel you are spiritually sick. Then, suddenly, a break in the clouds. 'A light surprises the Christian while he sings.' He was singing mechanically. The hymn had been given out and he just sang it with everybody else, not expecting anything to happen. But suddenly he feels he is illuminated.

> Sometimes a light surprises
>   The Christian while he sings;
> It is the Lord who rises
>   With healing in His wings;
> When comforts are declining,
>   He grants the soul again
> A season of clear shining
>   To cheer it after rain.

Do you know that? Does he surprise you in his visitations, in his intimations of his loving interest in you? Do you know what it is to be surprised by him? That is essential. It means that he has committed himself to you – you are in the relationship, and once you are in this relationship, he will act and will go on acting. He 'knocks at the door', as we are told in Revelation 3:20. He keeps on doing this, and he surprises us.

A *self* contained and a *self* controlled Christian life is a terrible thing: polite, nice, respectable. On Sunday morning you do your duty by going to church, but once a Sunday is quite enough – and so on. You handle everything. Oh, God, have mercy upon you! Has he ever committed himself to you at all? Do you know anything of these surprises, these touches, these visitations, these intimations, that you belong to him?

And then we must add the consciousness that we are being led on. There is no stagnation when he commits himself to us. Never! His leading is always progressive. He does not make us turn round in a circle, but takes us on. How do we know this? Here are the tests: Have you an increasing hunger for him? Have you an increasing longing within you to know him? Look at this man Paul at the height of his great achievement, having written these amazing epistles, and this is what he says: 'That I may know him, and the power of his resurrection, and the fellowship of his sufferings, being made conformable unto his death; if by any means I might attain unto the resurrection of the dead' (Philippians 3:10–11). That was Paul's greatest longing and desire. He knew his Lord, but he wanted to know him more! Is there a longing in you, an increasing thirst, for the living God? Is your heart panting after him increasingly? If so, you need not worry, he has committed himself to you.

Do you have an increasing enjoyment of spiritual things? Do you get increasing pleasure in the word of God, and in the preaching of the word of God, and the teaching of the word of God? Are these the things that ravish you more and more, so that you want more and more of them? Oh, that is an absolute proof that he has committed himself to you! Do you have an increasing desire to please him – not just to live a correct little evangelical life, but to please him in all things and to live to his glory? And then do you have an increasing love of the brethren, a delight in his people?

Finally, the topmost height of it all: 'The Spirit itself beareth witness with our spirit, that we are the children of God' (Romans 8:16). Hitherto I have suggested deductions, inferences you may have, and they are wonderful, thank God for them. But beyond all that it is possible to know what it is to have the Holy Spirit himself directly and immediately bearing witness with your spirit, and telling you that you are God's child. 'And if children, then heirs; heirs of God, and joint-heirs with Christ' (verse 17).

Has he committed himself to you? That is the crucial question.

11

The Temple of His Body

But he spake of the temple of his body.   John 2:21

Let me remind you of the context:

> Then answered the Jews and said unto him, What sign
> shewest thou unto us, seeing that thou doest these things?
> Jesus answered and said unto them, Destroy this temple,
> and in three days I will raise it up. Then said the Jews,
> Forty and six years was this temple in building, and wilt
> thou rear it up in three days? But he spake of the temple
> of his body. When therefore he was risen from the dead,
> his disciples remembered that he had said this unto them;
> and they believed the scripture, and the word which Jesus
> had said.   John 2:18–22

The Christmas season[1] is of value to us all because it
directs our attention to the person of our blessed Lord

---

[1] This sermon was preached on 19th December 1965.

and Saviour. There are pedants who try to tell us that we cannot be sure of the dates and that the observance of 25th December as Christmas day is the 'baptising', as they call it, of a pagan custom. But that does not make the slightest difference. What makes the whole difference to us is the great fact, the great event itself. The exact date is quite irrelevant. The important thing is that notable event which has changed the entire course of human history.

Also, as with no other teaching, the person is here not only central but absolutely vital. There are many religions in the world, many teachings, many of them associated with the names of particular men. But these men are not essential to them, somebody else might equally well have taught the same thing. To say that is not to detract from the greatness of the particular men, but they are not vital; it is the teaching that matters.

But in the Christian religion it is the person himself who counts. The teaching is all about him. Our view of him will therefore determine our view of the Christian faith, our view of salvation, indeed, our view of the whole world. So nothing is more important for us than to know exactly what we believe concerning him. The vital question facing men and women today was propounded by our Lord himself – 'What think ye of Christ?' (Matthew 22:42). Now there are only two main answers with regard to the great question: Who is Christ? And the view one holds of his birth is of direct relevance to the answer one gives. On the one hand, there are those who say that he was only a man and nothing more. A great man, they are prepared to grant, an unusual man, an outstanding man, but only a man.

Some are prepared to say that as the result of his good, faithful, obedient life he achieved divinity. Others say that because of the life he lived and the obedience that he rendered unto God, he became one through whom God could manifest himself to us, one with whom we can join, as it were, in obeying and worshipping God. Because of his outstanding godliness, it is said, God was able to use him in order to teach us things about himself. Others emphasise the point that he is one who helps make God real to us. But all these views have one thing in common: they regard him as but a man.

Those of you who are familiar with your Scriptures will know that there is nothing new about all this. This is something that has been said about him from the very beginning. With extraordinary honesty, the New Testament Gospels record that all these things were said about him from the moment of his birth until his ascension into heaven. But though this is nothing new, the world in its blindness and folly always gets excited about it, with people speaking in the name of 'scholar-ship' and so on.

Now let me take this opportunity of saying this about the so-called 'scholarship', at the sight of which some people always begin to tremble with alarm! Such scholarship possesses no special authority. It merely indicates that men and women have given their lives to doing a certain amount of work along a given line, but that does not endow them with any unusual faculties or powers. Furthermore, we need never be afraid of scholarship because it always cancels itself out. I know that newspapers give publicity to people who are unusually blatant in their opposition to the gospel;

they have always done that. That is what the world has always done. But these people do not possess any knowledge that no other people have, they do not have unusual powers, and there are scholars of equal standing who disagree with them entirely and deny everything that they say.

What I am trying to say is this: your faith and mine is not something that rests upon a shaky foundation. You need never be afraid that in a few years' time some old manuscripts will be unearthed, or somebody will make some wonderful discovery, and we will suddenly find that it has all been just a fairytale. That will never happen; it cannot happen. And if you are at all disturbed by this kind of thing, then I say that you really must learn the Scriptures and realise the arguments on which the fact of our Lord and who he was and what he did are so firmly based. We are not in any kind of precarious position.

Now I do not propose to put forward all the arguments, but I will give you just one. It is an argument that we can never repeat too frequently, and it is more than sufficient to prove my case. It is the argument of prophecy. You see, we are not dependent only upon what we are told in the New Testament, we have the Old Testament, and there in the Old Testament we read the prophecies concerning the One who was to come. Details are given, and those details were literally fulfilled and verified.

That is the answer – quite apart from the fact, of course, that anyone who can believe that the world for nearly twenty centuries has been believing a lie, can believe anything! The whole story of the Christian faith makes all these foolish denials which are put forward in the name of scholarship look quite ridiculous. There is, I repeat, nothing new about this. People have been doing this kind of thing throughout the centuries and they will continue to do so. But in the account of our Lord's birth we are reminded, and this is the importance of observing this particular season, of certain facts on which our faith is so solidly based.

So one view of our Lord is that he was only a man, that he himself had certain ideas, and his followers imagined various other things and concocted a story, writing down things which never happened in order to make him look great. That idea is reported fully in the New Testament itself. So the repetition of it at the present time should not trouble us in the slightest.

The other view is that this baby who was born in Bethlehem is the Son of God, the second Person in the blessed Holy Trinity. Now this is the great teaching of the New Testament and we either accept it or we do not. But if we do not, it means that we regard the apostles and other writers as frauds – indeed, they have been given the title of 'pious frauds'. But it is one or the other. We either believe the record and say, 'I cannot see how the Christian church could ever have come into being if these things were not true,' or else we agree with these so-called clever people. We either believe the record or we reject it.

Now the teaching concerning our Lord's divinity is given in many ways. We have these wonderful stories of the announcement of his birth, and of his birth in the stable. We are told about the shepherds, and Mary and Joseph, and the wise men. We read of the gladness and

the joy and the rejoicing and the singing in the heavenly
places. But in addition to all that, the Gospels give us
some explicit teaching, and it is to this that I want to
call your attention, especially as it is put in this twenty-
first verse of John chapter 2. After all, our business as
Christian people is not merely to record these things
and to remind ourselves of them, but to try to enter
more deeply into an understanding of them. To this
end, this phrase that is used here by John is most
illuminating.

John, as you remember, gives an account of the
cleansing of the Temple by our Lord at the time of the
Passover, and the response of the Jews to that. John
shows us how they challenged our Lord to give a striking, startling sign, and how he answers with the words,
'Destroy this temple, and in three days I will raise it
up.' The Jews are perplexed by this, and say, 'Forty and
six years was this temple in building, and wilt thou rear
it up in three days?' And John adds, for our clarifica-
tion, 'But he spake of the temple of his body.' And that
is a most illuminating phrase with regard to the birth of
our blessed Lord and Saviour.

Now the word 'temple' could be translated 'shrine':
'He spake of the shrine of his body.' Our Lord is
speaking here in an enigmatic manner. He is speaking
with a double meaning. He has just cleansed the literal,
physical temple, and everybody is thinking about that,
but he is also talking about his own body, and in doing
so he gives very wonderful teaching with regard to
what happened at the Incarnation. In other words, his
teaching is that the Temple in Jerusalem is nothing but
a type or a figure of his body. The people are all

thinking of the Jerusalem Temple, and he allows them to do so because he wants to show them the connection.

I referred earlier to the element of prophecy in the Old Testament, and we do not begin to understand the Old Testament unless we look at it in the light of the New Testament and its history, and see the way in which our Lord is the fulfilment of all the types and shadows that are recorded in the Old Testament. We are all familiar with some of them – the lamb and the burnt offerings and so on – but I think that sometimes we tend to forget that perhaps the greatest type of all was the Temple itself.

In the Old Testament we read how God first commanded his people to build a tabernacle in the wilderness. But the tabernacle was only the forerunner of the great Temple that was built in Jerusalem. We are given a detailed account of the measurements and the materials that were to go into the building of this Temple. We can picture all the gold, and the magnificence and the glory and the wonder of it all. Why all that detail? There is only one answer to that. The Temple prefigured the body into which the eternal Son of God would enter.

If you go back to the Old Testament and read some of the accounts of the building of the Temple, you will find that they are most illuminating. Read, for instance, Solomon's prayer at the dedication, the opening, of the Temple: 'But will God indeed dwell on the earth?' (2 Kings 8:27). Here Solomon is talking about the Temple, and in particular about that innermost part of the Temple called 'the Holiest of all', that place into which the high priest alone was allowed to enter and then only once a year, for there God has come down, as it were, to dwell. There is the ark of the covenant, the mercy seat, the cherubim covering the mercy seat, and there is the Shekinah glory, the emblem of the presence of God (verses 10–11).

Now Solomon has been prepared for all this by the instructions given to him. The great day of the opening comes, and this is how he speaks: 'But will God indeed dwell on the earth? behold, the heaven and heaven of heavens cannot contain thee; how much less this house that I have builded?' (verse 27). The Temple, and particularly that innermost shrine, was built to be the house of God, the place in which God would dwell.

Now in John 2 our Lord is confirming this teaching and explaining it. When he says, 'Destroy this temple, and in three days I will raise it up,' he is primarily referring, as John tells us, to his body. 'Destroy this, my body,' he says, 'and I will raise it up in three days.' But he knows that the Jews are thinking of the Temple in Jerusalem, and he is suggesting that they are right, that these two things go together.

So the light that this incident throws on the Incarnation is this: Jesus of Nazareth is God – God the eternal Son. And his body is the house in which he dwells. The body of that infant, that babe lying in the manger, is but the dwelling place of the eternal God in the person of the Son.

We have this same idea in John 1:14: 'The Word was made flesh, and dwelt among us,' which should be translated, 'The Word was made flesh and tabernacled among us.' That is referring to the fact that the body of our Lord, like the body of each of us, is nothing but a

kind of tent in which we spend a certain amount of
time in this world. But it does carry the further idea of
the place where God comes down, as it were, to dwell.
What the tabernacle and the Temple were to the living
God under the old dispensation, so the body of Jesus
Christ is to him in the new dispensation.

We find the same idea in Colossians 2:9, which is
most wonderful teaching. We should be keeping this in
our minds as we think of the Incarnation: 'For in him
dwelleth all the fulness of the Godhead bodily.' The
fullness of the Godhead is all in this temple, this body.
'It pleased the Father that in him should all fulness
dwell' (Colossians 1:19).

Another way of looking at this is given in a prophecy
in Isaiah 7 about the birth of our Lord. Isaiah
prophesies that he will be born of a virgin, and the
prophecy goes on to say, '. . . and shall call his name
Immanuel' (Isaiah 7:14). Matthew quotes this verse
from Isaiah, and adds, 'which being interpreted is, God
with us' (Matthew 1:23).

And that is what we see there in the stable in
Bethlehem – 'God with us', God dwelling with us in
that particular form. Or, to take it further, we can put
it like this: as in the Temple of old, and in the Holiest
of all, God's presence dwelt, and man, represented by
the high priest, went in and met with God, so now the
meeting place between God and humanity is in this
temple in which the eternal Son dwells. The meeting
place is the Lord Jesus Christ himself. So when our
Lord talks about the temple of his body, he is saying:
What the Temple was, I am. This body is the temple. I
am the eternal Son of God dwelling in this temple. This

is the place where man now meets with God.

So it is not surprising that later on our Lord said, 'He who hath seen me hath seen the Father' (John 14:9). The everlasting and eternal God is dwelling here in the person of the Son in this tent, in this tabernacle. In Paul's words, 'Great is the mystery of godliness.' What is it? 'God was manifest in the flesh' (1 Timothy 3:16).

That is what Christmas means; that is what the birth of that child in Bethlehem means. In the old Temple God was manifest in the Shekinah glory. But now God is manifest in flesh and blood, in human form, in a child lying in a manger. So that the little children's hymn is quite right:

> I love to hear the story
> Which angel voices tell,
> How once the King of Glory
> Came down on earth to dwell.
> *Emily Huntington Miller*

So, here in John 2, our Lord, in speaking in this enigmatic manner, is throwing light upon the great event which took place, throwing light upon the meaning of the Incarnation.

But let us go on and look at the element of mystery in the Incarnation, a mystery which is apparent in this very incident in John 2. There is a double meaning here, and that is why these people were confused and missed it. While he was here on earth, most people missed it. The Pharisees and scribes never recognised him. They heard him speaking, they saw his miracles, they questioned him and he was never at a loss in the matter of answering them, and yet they never saw him. They saw nothing but a carpenter, nothing but Jesus, the one whom they felt was an imposter, one whom they hated, and eventually crucified. As usual, the apostle Paul sums it all up for us. In 1 Corinthians 2:8 he says, 'Which none of the princes of this world knew: for had they known it, they would not have crucified the Lord of glory.'

The cleverest people of the world have never recognised him. They only see the temple, they do not see the person dwelling in it. They see the external, they miss the real glory and marvel and mystery. And I feel that John has added this verse because you and I are liable to do the same thing. So he helps us by saying, 'He spake of the temple of his body,' and we must be clear that we understand this.

This is a mystery, a marvel. It is wonderful and miraculous. It is supernatural and beyond understanding. And if we could only see it, the more these clever modern people fumble at this and stumble at it, the more we should be certain. The princes of this world have never known him and never will. They are blinded by prejudice. They do not want to know. They call themselves great and learned and wonderful scholars, but it is all blindness. The world has never recognised him because of this mystery and marvel.

This is what makes Christmas for those of us who are Christians. 'No man hath seen God at any time' (John 1:18). God is Spirit.

> Immortal, invisible, God only wise,
> In light inaccessible hid from our eyes.
>   *Walter Chalmers Smith*

That is God, 'dwelling in the light which no man can approach unto; whom no man hath seen, nor can see' (1 Timothy 6:16). And yet we are told that the babe lying in the manger is Eternal God the Son. It is not surprising, is it, that people stumble at it? The thing is incredible to the natural human mind and intellect. So the great apostle himself has to say, 'Great is the mystery of godliness' (1 Timothy 3:16). The world ridicules a thing like this. Of course it does, because it is so entirely beyond its understanding. Foolish man measures everything by his own feeble and imperfect understanding.

So we must look at the Incarnation again. People miss its significance because they do not look at it in the light of our Lord's words here at the end of John 2. Look at the confining that took place in his person. Solomon said, 'Will God indeed dwell on the earth?' Is this possible? Can it happen in this confined space? 'Behold,' he says, 'the heaven and heaven of heavens cannot contain thee; how much less this house that I have builded?' (1 Kings 8:27). But remember that the house Solomon had built, and Herod was rebuilding, was a very big house, a spacious building. It was large and imposing, one of the great buildings of the world.

But wait a minute! We are looking at a little helpless babe lying in a manger. Is it possible that 'all the fulness of the Godhead' can be confined to that little body? It is true. That is exactly what happened. This is the temple. You are looking at the temple in which he, the eternal Son of God, came to dwell. And therefore the apostle says, 'In him' – in that babe – 'dwelleth all the fulness of the Godhead bodily.' The compression, the confining

– here is a part of the marvel and the mystery.

Or look at another aspect of it. In that one baby there are two natures. There is only one person, he is Jesus, but there are two natures in him. He is God; he is man. He is divine; he is human. And to heighten the marvel and the mystery, these two natures, though they are resident in the one person, are not blended. They are not intermingled. Man! God! Both perfect, both absolute, both real, and both unmixed. It is not surprising, is it, that the clever people do not accept this? 'Oh,' they say, 'but I cannot understand it.' Of course not!

And where the world shows itself to be such a fool is that it even tries to understand. We are not talking about things that can be understood but about the most shattering thing that has ever happened in the world. The creation of the world at the beginning is nothing in comparison with this. This is the mightiest thing of all – God coming down, being confined to that little body. Perfect man. Perfect God. Both real, both separate, both distinct, yet both together forming this one person.

Or take another aspect, and again this is something that has confused people. As we read the Gospels we always find that at one and the same time there is a manifesting and a hiding, a revelation and a concealing. We see it in this one incident in John 2. Here are these people, very interested in the material Temple, and our Lord says, 'Destroy this temple, and in three days I will raise it up again.' As we saw earlier, there is a mystery here. He is saying something about himself, and yet he may not be. He may be talking about the Temple only, or yet he may be talking about himself, or talking about both at the same time.

This is typical of how he went on throughout his life in this world. There is a manifesting of a glory; there is a concealing of a glory. And that is why people were always divided into two groups when they came into contact with him. As we have been seeing, there were people like the disciples and others who sensed something, who felt something, who saw some glimmer of the glory that was there. But others saw nothing but the temple, the body, the outward appearance.

'No man hath seen God at any time,' said John (John 1:18). And we read in Exodus, 'There shall no man see me, and live,' said God himself to Moses (Exodus 33:20). We cannot 'see' the Godhead in its fullness, it would kill us. So as Charles Wesley puts it in the famous hymn: 'Veiled in flesh the Godhead see.' If you have eyes to see, you will see the glory streaming forth. If you have not, you will see nothing but the flesh, the veiling, the concealing.

Again, there is the extraordinary combination of power and weakness. We see the power of the miracles, turning water into wine at Cana of Galilee, cleansing the Temple by the authority of his word. And we see the power of his knowledge – as we are told here in John 2: 'Jesus did not commit himself unto them, because he knew all men, and needed not that any should testify of man: for he knew what was in man.' Yet there are times in the Gospels when he does not seem to know. There are times when he seems to be just a man. He exerts his authority and power: he can quell the raging of the sea, he can raise the dead, yet he dies and is crucified in apparent weakness. Here is the mystery. Here is the enigma. Here is the marvel. Here is the wonder of it all. And these are but expressions of the central mystery. 'Veiled in flesh the Godhead see.' 'The Word was made flesh, and dwelt among us.' It is the greatest marvel, the greatest mystery of all.

But, finally, look at what we are told here about the message of the Incarnation. After all, this is our real interest, is it not? The test of whether or not we are Christians at a time like this is the way we look at these events. Is Christmas just a time to send Christmas cards to one another and to sing carols? The world has gone mad on singing, and the more it sings the less it thinks. But you and I are meant to think, and to discover the meaning of all this, and here we are told the meaning and it is very clear.

You must not stop at the babe in the manger. Our Lord himself will not allow us to stop at that. The birth is but a means to an end. Here he is at the very beginning of his ministry, and this is what he says: 'Destroy this temple' – break down my body – 'and in three days I will raise it again.' This is a clear prophecy of his death and resurrection. And that, of course, is why he came into the world. He did not come merely to give us a spectacle, or teaching, or an example. We must never lose sight of the fact that he entered into this world, he broke into time, he was born as a baby in a stable and put into the manger, in order that he might die.

The great statement of this is in Hebrews 2. 'But now we see not yet all things put under him. But we see Jesus, who was made a little lower than the angels for the suffering of death, crowned with glory and honour;

that he by the grace of God should taste death for every man' (Hebrews 2:8–9). He was made 'a little lower than the angels'. That is it! He was born as a babe in Bethlehem, and a babe is a little lower than the angels. He had made the angels – it does not matter. He himself is now made a little lower than the angels. What for? 'For the suffering of death'! He came into the temple in order that the temple might be destroyed. He entered into this building in order that the building might be drawn apart, might be separated, as it were, might be broken down. So this is the great thing on which we must always live and dwell. We cannot be saved by fairytales. Of course not. We are not dealing with one. We are told of One who was born in order that he might die, and rise again, and conquer all our enemies.

But why did he do all this? Why did he come? And in a very wonderful way this statement in John 2:20 answers the question. He came in order to introduce a new way for men and women to know God. He came to introduce a new covenant, a new dispensation. His body was destroyed, as he prophesied it would be. But the Temple also was destroyed, and that is where these two things are interrelated. In effect, he is saying: 'If you destroy this temple, you are at the same time destroying that Temple.' And that is the very thing that happened. When our Lord was dying on the cross, the veil of the Temple was 'rent in twain' (Matthew 27:51). The veil, the curtain that separated off the Holiest of all from the sight of men and women, was torn in two. The Holiest of all became open. In AD 70 the whole grand edifice, the Temple and all its courts, was destroyed and reduced to a mass of rubble.

When our Lord cleansed the Temple, the people were upset and annoyed and said, 'Who are you? What right have you?' And he replied in effect: 'You do not know me. You do not understand. You do not realise that I am the new temple. There is to be a destruction. You will destroy me, my body, as it were, because you do not understand me. But you are doing more than you know; you will also be destroying a dispensation.'

That is why he came into the world. He came to put an end to the old dispensation. The Temple was destroyed, and for ever. To the Jews, the Temple was everything. They thought that it was theirs. So he wanted to teach them that the Temple was only temporary. There would be no restoration of the Temple in Jerusalem, no bringing back of the ceremonial and the ritual and the Old Testament worship. He came to put an end to that, and he did, once and for ever, by the destruction of his own body.

But he also taught that he would erect a new temple. The whole object of the Incarnation was to provide for us a new place in which to meet with God. The meeting place is no longer in the man-made Temple. God 'dwelleth not in temples made with hands' (Acts 17:24). We meet him in the person of his Son, the One who came to the temple of his body, whose body was raised. And he has taken back his body. He is still in it. He is the only place where we can meet with God. He is the propitiation. He is the High Priest. He is the All and in all. And so he said, 'I am the way, the truth, and the life: no man cometh unto the Father, but by me' (John 14:6). We do not meet God any longer in temples.

We do not find the way to him by 'the blood of bulls and of goats, and the ashes of an heifer' (Hebrews 9:13). No, no; it is all in Christ, in this one person. The old Temple was but the picture. The Holiest of all in the old Temple was but the prefiguring. Now it is in Christ, and in him alone, that God and man meet, 'God and sinner reconciled'. The meeting-place of heaven and earth, of the human and the divine, is all in this one blessed person. 'He spake of the temple of his body.'

And then, lastly, as the result of his work, we are entitled to go on and to say that you and I are now the temple. The Lord Jesus Christ now dwells in the church, and the church is the temple. The Christian church replaces the old Temple in Jerusalem. That is why the notion held by some foolish people that the Temple will be rebuilt and blood offerings and sacrifices restored is a denial of the New Testament gospel.

Let me give you the evidence for saying this. Paul says, 'Know ye not that ye are the temple of God, and that the Spirit of God dwelleth in you? If any man defile the temple of God, him shall God destroy; for the temple of God is holy, which temple ye are' (1 Corinthians 3:16–17). Our Lord came down and dwelt in a body. He has come again and he dwells in us by the Spirit. Or take 1 Corinthians 6:19: 'What? know ye not that your body is the temple of the Holy Ghost . . . ?' We find the same at the end of Ephesians 1: 'And hath put all things under his feet, and gave him to be the head over all things to the church, which is his body, the fulness of him that filleth all in all' (Ephesians 1:22–23).

Or take the end of Ephesians 2: 'And are built upon the foundation of the apostles and prophets, Jesus Christ himself being the chief corner stone; in whom all the building fitly framed together groweth unto an holy temple in the Lord: in whom ye also are builded together for an habitation of God through the Spirit' (Ephesians 2:20–22). We are the habitation of God, the temple of God. Indeed, you remember how in the fourteenth chapter of this Gospel of John, our Lord puts it like this: 'If a man love me, he will keep my words: and my Father will love him, and we will come unto him, and make our abode with him' (verse 23).

These are the results of the Incarnation – no longer an external temple, he has done away with that; no longer the temple of his body while here on earth. The church is now the temple in which he dwells. Yes, and beyond that, you and I as Christian people are the temple in which he takes up his abode by the Spirit. There is nothing more wonderful and more thrilling for us to be aware of concerning ourselves. Oh, the marvel, the wonder, the mystery, the miracle, the glory of it all! May God give us increasing understanding of all these things. Above all, may he enable us to realise that as members of the Christian church we are part of this temple in which he dwells, and that in us individually he comes to dwell by faith.

He and the Father take up their abode in us. All that would have been impossible were it not for the birth of the Son of God as the babe of Bethlehem.

12

The Captain's Inspection

Now when he was in Jerusalem at the passover, in the feast day, many believed in his name, when they saw the miracles which he did. But Jesus did not commit himself unto them, because he knew all men, and needed not that any should testify of man: for he knew what was in man.   John 2:23–25

We have spent some time in examining ourselves in order to discover whether or not our Lord has committed himself unto us and now I want to take a further step and raise a subject which it is very appropriate for us to consider on this, the last Sunday of an old year.[1] Here we have a picture of the Lord Jesus Christ standing and looking at people, and not merely looking at them, but judging them, assessing them and determining their fate. And I want to hold this idea before you because it is true for all of us. The Scriptures exhort us

---

[1] This sermon was preached on 26th December 1965.

to examine ourselves, it is very right and proper that we should do so constantly. But much more important than our self-examination is the realisation that he looks upon us and examines us and we have no choice in this matter. The Scriptures describe our Lord as 'the captain of our salvation': 'For it became him, for whom are all things, and by whom are all things, in bringing many sons unto glory, to make the captain of their salvation perfect through suffering' (Hebrews 2:10). We find the same idea in the twelfth chapter: he is 'the author and finisher of our faith' (Hebrews 12:2), which could be translated 'the leader', 'file-leader', if you like, the one who goes ahead, the one in charge.

Here, then, is the Captain of our salvation looking at men and women. This is something that he does to all and with all. And I suggest that there are three main aspects of this inspection. He inspects us as we join; he continues to inspect us while we are serving, especially on certain occasions; and there is to be a final inspection.

You cannot enter into the Christian life without his choosing you. That is what lies here on the very surface of this verse – as we have already seen. These people, impressed, moved, carried away by the miracles, are anxious to follow him. But he does not receive them. Of course, all Christians have a desire to follow him. I do not wish to emphasise that at the moment, but to impress upon us that our desire alone is not sufficient. We have his great word, and thank God for it: 'Him that cometh to me I will in no wise cast out' (John 6:37), and yet he does not receive these people who do come to him.

So there is a coming and a coming. The ones he receives and to whom he says, 'Him that cometh unto me I will in no wise cast out,' are those who are called of God, and he knows them. But think of a soldier joining an army. Before he is accepted, that soldier must undergo an inspection, an examination. So with you as a Christian, you cannot just walk in and out whenever you like. As you come to him, he looks at you, he inspects you. And it is his prerogative and his right as the Captain of salvation to accept or to reject according to his holy will. Therefore we can be quite confident that if we are Christians, then he has looked at us, examined us, and accepted us. Here he is, looking at people. They come, yes, but what matters is the way that he looks at them.

But as the Captain of our salvation, he not only inspects us at the very beginning when we enlist, as it were, but keeps on doing so. And there are special times when he does this in an unusual manner. He reviews his troops; he commands a kind of parade, and we have to appear before him. We are regularly performing our various duties as soldiers in the Christian army, but from time to time he announces that there is to be a general inspection of the troops. And I always feel that the end of a year is one such occasion.

Let us, then, look at this second type of inspection, the one that takes place constantly but which he initiates now and again in a special way. The important thing for us here is to realise the truth concerning him and his characteristics as the Reviewer of the troops, and that is what is emphasised here: 'Jesus did not commit himself unto them, because he knew all men, and needed not that any should testify of man: for he knew what was in man.' He does not need to be prompted by any assistants. He does not need to have them whispering into his ear about this person or that person; it is unnecessary. He looks and he sees. He knows everything and comes to certain conclusions.

Let us, then, for our good and our encouragement, concentrate on our Lord's all-seeing eye. What are some of the many things that we find in the Scriptures about his 'examining eye'? The first is that it is a discerning eye, an eye which cannot be misled. This is a sobering thought but it comes out everywhere in the Bible. The perfect example is in this incident in the Temple at Jerusalem at the time of the Passover. You and I see people and draw our conclusions, but we are so often wrong because we lack discernment. Our Lord has a discerning eye. He does not commit himself to them. He does commit himself to others.

We see this in the case of the people whom our Lord describes at the end of the Sermon on the Mount. He talks about people who come to him at the end and say: 'Lord, Lord, have we not . . . in thy name done many wonderful works?' (Matthew 7:22). But his answer is: 'I never knew you' (verse 23). He has looked at them but has never committed himself to them.

Perhaps one of the most striking examples of this discernment is in the case of the so-called 'rich young ruler', that young man who came eagerly to our Lord saying, 'What shall I do that I may inherit eternal life?' (Mark 10:17) – and he was a noble and a beautiful and an excellent young man. We are told, 'Then Jesus beholding him loved him' (verse 21) – which means that our Lord saw at a glance that young man's excellent qualities. So you would have thought that here was the kind of person whom our Lord would receive and who would spend the rest of his life with him.

But that did not happen. 'Jesus said unto him, Why callest thou me good? there is none good but one, that is, God. Thou knowest the commandments . . . Honour thy father and mother . . .' And the young man was able to say, 'All these have I observed from my youth.' Then the significant statement follows: 'Jesus beholding him loved him, and said unto him, One thing thou lackest' (Mark 10:18–21). And thereby our Lord revealed that he knew the real secret of this young man and his problem, that though he was beautiful to look at, though he was moral, though he was excellent and good in so many ways, there was one thing wrong. It does not matter what it was – in that particular case it was a love of money, not the possession of it but the love of it. So our Lord said to him, 'Go thy way, sell whatsoever thou hast, and give to the poor, and thou shalt have treasure in heaven: and come, take up the cross and follow me' (Mark 10:21). The Lord was able to discern this, and that is something that always stands out in all these descriptions that we have of him.

Let me take that further by describing this eye of his as not only discerning, but searching. It is, of course, discerning because it is searching. Everywhere in the Bible this is what is emphasised about God the Father, and about God the Son, and about God the Holy Spirit. David, for instance, comes to a realisation of this and expresses it in Psalm 51 when he says, 'Thou desirest truth in the inward parts' (verse 6); not on the lips, but in the 'inward parts'. David is in trouble. He has sinned, and he knows that he has sinned, against God. He is not worried about what men may think of him but he is very concerned about what God may think, and here is his problem: 'Thou desirest truth in the inward parts.' And again in Psalm 139, the psalmist says the same thing: 'Thou knowest my downsitting and mine uprising, thou understandest my thought afar off' (verse 2).

Here is something which is emphasised constantly about our Lord. He even says it himself. He turned to the Pharisees and the scribes one day and said, 'Ye are they which justify yourselves before men; but God knoweth your hearts: and that which is highly esteemed among men is abomination in the sight of God' (Luke 16:15). Why? Well, the difference is this: people judge by outward appearance, and that is why the Jews revered the Pharisees and the scribes – good men, moral men, religious men. 'They make broad their phylacteries' (Matthew 23:5). Looking at and inspecting them in general you might award them a hundred per cent, full marks. Ah, but, 'God seeth the heart.' He does not merely see the external appearance, he sees the heart, and, 'That which is highly esteemed among men is abomination in the sight of God.' When he was teaching in the Temple, our Lord put it in a great principle: 'Judge not according to the appearance, but judge righteous judgment' (John 7:24).

This is expressed in a striking and alarming manner in the fourth chapter of the epistle to the Hebrews:

For the word of God is quick, and powerful, and sharper than any twoedged sword, piercing even to the dividing asunder of soul and spirit, and of the joints and marrow, and is a discerner of the thoughts and intents of the heart. Neither is there any creature that is not manifest in his sight: but all things are naked and opened unto the eyes of him with whom we have to do.   Hebrews 4:12–13

That is it: his glance is searching. It sees everything, not merely the outward appearance but the depth of the heart, the vitals of one's entire being.

Now that tends to fill us with a good deal of alarm and terror. Who can bear this searching sight, this penetrating glance? But, thank God, that is not all that we are told about the way in which he looks. Next there is what I can only describe as 'the chiding eye'. He looks at us and at times he chides us. I am not saying 'condemning eye' because there is an admixture of condemnation and yet of pity. We must take our Lord as he is – thank God we must do so, otherwise we would all be undone. If we were to stop at his discernment, we would all be condemned, but there is this further element.

A supreme example is seen in the case of the apostle Peter. Towards the end, when our Lord began to make it clear to the disciples that he would be arrested and tried, Peter as usual in his impulsive manner said: Though all men leave you and deny you, I will not (see Matthew 26:33, Luke 22:33). Peter was prepared to follow his Lord anywhere, even through death. But when our Lord was arrested, this is what we read:

Then took they him, and led him, and brought him into the high priest's house. And Peter followed afar off. And when they had kindled a fire in the midst of the hall, and were set down together, Peter sat down among them. But a certain maid beheld him as he sat by the fire, and earnestly looked upon him, and said, This man was also with him. And he denied him, saying, Woman, I know him not. And after a little while another saw him, and said, Thou art also of them. And Peter said, Man, I am not. And about the space of one hour after another confidently affirmed, saying, Of a truth this fellow also was with him: for he is a Galilaean. And Peter said, Man, I know not what thou sayest. And immediately, while he yet spake, the cock crew.   Luke 22:54–60

You see the significance of that? When Peter made his boastful statement our Lord said, 'Before the cock crow, thou shalt deny me thrice.'

And the Lord turned, and looked upon Peter. And Peter remembered the word of the Lord, how he had said unto him, Before the cock crow, thou shalt deny me thrice. And Peter went out, and wept bitterly.   verses 61–62

Now this same blessed Lord is looking at us one by one. We claim to be his people, we are his followers, we belong to him, we have been with him, we have accompanied him, we have said things to him, but he is looking at us and I wonder if any of us feel as Peter felt? He knows us so well. When Peter was boasting and bragging in his typical manner our Lord knew it was all empty. He knew the man. When Peter denied him for the third time, our Lord did not say anything. We read, 'The Lord turned, and looked upon Peter.'

Do you recognise the look in his eye? What is he

saying to you? Are we conscious of being chided, of being reminded of things we have professed, and things we have claimed, and things we have said? Are we aware of the contrast between our words and our behaviour? We can be quite certain that as he turned and looked upon Peter on that occasion, and as he looked at those people who were there before him in Jerusalem, so he is looking upon us.

But that leads me to the next point, and thank God for this; even at that desperate moment there was hope in the look which our Lord gave there to Peter. 'Peter went out, and wept bitterly' (Luke 22:62). Yes, he did that because he saw something beyond condemnation in that look, he saw pity; he saw compassion. That is the difference between a Peter and a Judas. Judas went out and hanged himself. There was no hope. He did not see what Peter saw. Judas did not see what I call our Lord's 'piteous eye'. There is a hymn which puts this very well:

> He hath, with a piteous eye,
> Looked upon our misery:
> For His mercies aye endure,
> Ever faithful, ever sure.
> *John Milton*

My dear, good friend, were it not for this piteous eye, we would not be considering this now. There would be no such thing as Christmas day. There would be nothing to celebrate. It is because he has a piteous eye that the Son of God ever came into this world.

Have you ever realised that our Lord's pity is the

whole basis of our salvation? It is put before us in many places. I always feel that one of the most wonderful and the most beautiful of all the accounts of God's compassion is found way back in the book of Exodus, where we are told of how it was that God ever called Moses and told him what to do. It is the essence of the statement that was made to Moses at the burning bush: 'And the Lord said, I have surely seen the affliction of my people which are in Egypt, and have heard their cry by reason of their taskmasters; for I know their sorrows; and I am come down to deliver them out of the hand of the Egyptians, and to bring them up out of that land unto a good land and a large, unto a land flowing with milk and honey . . .' (Exodus 3:7–8). But the significant statement is: 'I have surely seen the affliction of my people.'

This is an anthropomorphism, of course. It is a picture of God looking down, as it were, from heaven upon the affliction of his people in Egypt. They are suffering under the taskmasters, and the lashes of their whips. They are in agony and feel they are finished. They remember the great promises made to their forefathers, but here it all seems to be denied. Everything is going against them. But suddenly this word is given to Moses. God has been watching it all – 'I have seen the affliction of my people.' God sees with an eye of pity, of compassion, of mercy. And as we read the Gospels this strikes us frequently. We are told that he looked upon the multitude with compassion because he saw them as sheep without a shepherd (see Mark 6:34 and Matthew 9:36). What a comforting, what a blessed thought that is!

He looks upon this world in a way that nobody else

can. Statesmen look upon the world and its peoples and their problems, but they do not look as he does. 'When he saw the multitude, he was moved with compassion' (Matthew 9:36). That is why he began to act. That is why he came into this world. That is why he ever went to the cross, and was buried. That is why he rose again.

We constantly find something like this in the Gospels: someone is in need or is suffering, and the disciples are intending to pass on by. But then we read, 'When Jesus saw him he had compassion upon him,' or, 'Jesus stopped, and looked upon him.' Our Lord never saw a case of suffering but that he had compassion and was always ready to do something by way of relief. And this is the one thing that comforts us and encourages us today. We look at ourselves as we see ourselves inspected by him, and suddenly we become aware of our imperfections and all the things we have not done, and we feel that we are about to be dismissed. But, let us remember, there is this other aspect, there is this pitying element.

We sometimes sing a hymn which begins:

> At even, ere the sun was set,
> The sick, O Lord, around Thee lay.

A couplet in this hymn goes:

> Thy kind but searching glance can scan
> The very wounds that shame would hide.
> *Henry Twells*

That is a tremendous statement, and it is one which is

very comforting for us. Maybe you are aware of something in your life which is filling you with a sense of shame. There is a wound, and that sense of shame causes you to hide it. But he sees it, and he looks on it – blessed be his name – with this eye of pity and of mercy and of compassion. His eye is kind as well as searching. What a combination! Thank God that it can heal the wounds as well as scan them.

So remember, as you feel that he is looking at you, that, 'He knoweth our frame; he remembereth that we are dust' (Psalm 103:14). Our Lord did not reject Peter when he denied him. He knew and made allowances for him. In the last chapter of John's Gospel we see how he dealt with Peter. O yes, he did, as it were, put him through it, and Peter felt a miserable worm, but still our Lord gave him the commission: 'Feed my lambs; feed my sheep.' He looked with this eye of pity and compassion.

But let me add one other characteristic to the way in which our Lord looks at us, and that is that there is a very surprising element about it. The result of the inspection is not always what we would expect it to be. And thank God, I say once more, for this. He reverses our decisions. Christian people can be divided into two main groups: those who never examine themselves at all, and those who do nothing but examine themselves and keep themselves in a perpetual state of misery. The first need to be made miserable; the second need to be comforted. And the Scriptures deal with both groups. I have been reminding you of his piercing glance, his knowledge of everything, and his compassion, but let us look at the surprising element.

We read in one of our Lord's own parables:

When the Son of man shall come in his glory, and all the holy angels with him, then shall he sit upon the throne of his glory: and before him shall be gathered all nations: and he shall separate them one from another, as a shepherd divideth his sheep from the goats: and he shall set the sheep on his right hand, but the goats on the left. Then shall the King say unto them on his right hand, Come, ye blessed of my Father, inherit the kingdom prepared for you from the foundation of the world: for I was an hungred, and ye gave me meat: I was thirsty, and ye gave me drink: I was a stranger, and ye took me in: naked, and ye clothed me: I was sick, and ye visited me: I was in prison, and ye came unto me. Then shall the righteous answer him, saying, Lord, when saw we thee an hungred, and fed thee? or thirsty, and gave thee drink? When saw we thee a stranger, and took thee in? or naked, and clothed thee? or when saw we thee sick, or in prison, and came unto thee? And the King shall answer and say unto them, Verily, I say unto you, Inasmuch as ye have done it unto one of the least of these my brethren, ye have done it unto me.   Matthew 25:31–40

But there is another side to that picture:

Then shall he say also unto them on the left hand, Depart from me, ye cursed, into everlasting fire, prepared for the devil and his angels: for I was an hungred, and ye gave me no meat: I was thirsty, and ye gave me no drink: I was a stranger, and ye took me not in: naked, and ye clothed me not: sick, and in prison, and ye visited me not. Then shall they also answer him, saying, Lord, when saw we thee an hungred . . .? Then shall he answer them, saying, Verily I say unto you, Inasmuch as ye did it not to one of the least of these, ye did it not to me. And these shall go away into everlasting punishment: but the righteous into life eternal.

Matthew 25:41–46

There may be some reading this who feel discouraged. You feel that you are useless and worthless, that you have done nothing. The devil has been tempting you to think that you are not a Christian at all. I am happy to believe, my dear friend, that if you feel like that about yourself you probably belong to this first group, the group on the right-hand side. And when he comes to look at you, you will have the surprise of your life for he will say, 'Come, ye blessed of my Father, inherit the kingdom prepared for you from the foundation of the world.' Thank God that he looks at us like this and that, as William Cowper put it, the needy soul finds:

> A season of clear shining,
> To cheer it after rain.

We quoted the hymn earlier:

> Sometimes a light surprises
>   The Christian while he sings;
> It is the Lord who rises
>   With healing in His wings.

I do trust that he is looking at you in this way. You have been down and the devil has depressed you. But as our Lord looks at you, do you not behold that smile? Do you not hear him saying to you, 'Come, you belong to me. Do not listen to the devil, listen to what I am saying to you.' There is a 'surprising' look in his eye, and it is his own people alone who know what it is like. There is nothing more wonderful than when you have been hiding yourself from him, as it were, afraid to look at him, but at last in desperation you just have to look up, and you see the most surprising thing you have ever seen. There is a look of love. There is a look of compassion and of mercy and of pity and of welcome, and you see this great invitation, 'Come!' And you go back to him, filled with 'joy unspeakable and full of glory' (1 Peter 1:8).

There, then, are the great things for us to realise, and, therefore, I would ask you: How do you feel as you examine yourself in this way? That is the great question for each of us. If you feel under condemnation, thank God we are given abundant instruction in the Scriptures as to what we must do about it – simply acknowledge it and repent. If necessary weep, as Peter wept of old when the Lord turned and looked upon him. Our Lord knows your heart. He knows that though you may have failed him, you did not want to, in a sense. It was your weakness that made you do it. And he hears you saying:

> Lord, it is my chief complaint
> That my love is weak and faint;
> Yet I love Thee, and adore;
> O for grace to love Thee more!
> *William Cowper*

Tell him that and he will hear you. He will receive you and heal you.

Listen to the way in which John puts this:

These things have I written unto you concerning them that seduce you. But the anointing which ye have received of him abideth in you, and ye need not that any man teach you: but as the same anointing teacheth you of all things, and is truth, and is no lie, and even as it hath taught you, ye shall abide in him. And now, little children, abide in him; that, when he shall appear, we may have confidence, and not be ashamed before him at his coming.

1 John 2:26–28

Thank God for this review, for this inspection. He is giving us a chance. He is telling us: This is only preliminary. I am coming again for a final inspection. I have looked at you: you feel unworthy? Very well, put yourself right. Repent. Acknowledge it all. Confess it all. Then, 'abide in him', and go on serving him truly, so that when he comes you will not in any sense be ashamed.

Or let me put it in terms of what he himself says to the church at Laodicea. The Christians in Laodicea thought they were rich and had need of nothing. But he says: I looked at you, and you do not know that you are 'wretched, and miserable, and poor, and blind, and naked' (Revelation 3:17). Do you feel like that? Do you feel 'poor, wretched, blind, naked'? Very well, he says, 'I counsel thee to buy of me gold tried in the fire, that thou mayest be rich; and white raiment, that thou mayest be clothed, and that the shame of thy nakedness do not appear; and anoint thine eyes with eyesalve, that thou mayest see. As many as I love, I rebuke and chasten' (Revelation 3:18–19).

If he is rebuking you and chastening you, it is because he loves you. Take his advice and buy this gold which you can have for nothing, and the raiment and the eyesalve, and go on and serve him and follow him for the remainder of your days in this world of time.

Above all, we must never cease to remember that his eye is always upon us. Always. Wherever we are, whatever we do, whatever we think or say, his eye is upon us. If only we remembered that! The most important resolution we can take, therefore, all of us, as we face a new year, is the resolution to remember that we are always walking under his eye.

> Leave no unguarded place,
>   No weakness of the soul,
> Take every virtue, every grace,
>   And fortify the whole.
> To keep your armour bright
>   Attend with constant care,
> Still walking in your Captain's sight,
>   And watching unto prayer.
>   *Charles Wesley*

Now there is the exact prescription. We really do not need to know anything beyond that.

So finally I ask you an ultimate question, the question of questions. How do you feel when you think about the final inspection? How do you feel as you think of the day when the trumpets and bugles will be sounding, and the grand parade will be held of the whole of humanity? How do you feel when you contemplate that parade which nobody can evade? You may refrain from going to chapel or church on Sunday; you may make your excuses. But no excuses will be accepted on that day. Everybody will be on parade, and the Captain himself will inspect us all. 'For,' says Paul, 'we must all appear before the judgment seat of Christ; that every one may receive the things done in his body according to that he hath done, whether it be good or bad' (2 Corinthians 5:10). That applies to believers as well as to non-believers.

We read in Revelation: 'Behold, he cometh with clouds; and every eye shall see him' (Revelation 1:7) – which means that everyone in the whole universe will see him looking into his or her eyes. And the great question is: How shall we feel?

Do not forget the description that we are given of him. 'His head and his hairs were white like wool, as white as snow; and his eyes were as a flame of fire' (Revelation 1:14). The eyes of holiness, the eyes of absolute purity – those are the eyes we shall all see. How do you feel as you contemplate that?

There is only one of two possibilities for every one of us. We are told in the sixth chapter of the book of Revelation how some people will feel. These are the people who did not believe in him, who laughed at his virgin birth, and ridiculed the idea that he had worked miracles, who scorned the blood of his cross as the only way of atonement, the substitutionary penal atonement, who ridiculed it all and denied the Resurrection, and the person of the Spirit. But they will see him: 'Every eye shall see him; yea, and they that pierced him.' And this will be the reaction:

And the kings of the earth, and the great men, and the rich men, and the chief captains, and the mighty men, and every bondman, and every free man, hid themselves in the dens and in the rocks of the mountains; and said to the mountains and rocks, Fall on us, and hide us from the face of him that sitteth on the throne, and from the wrath of the Lamb: for the great day of his wrath is come; and who shall be able to stand? Revelation 6:15–17

They see nothing but the fire of his wrath against all sin and evil and iniquity.

Oh, I am happy to believe that that is not going to be your position nor mine. Ours, rather, is this, is it not: 'Behold, what manner of love the Father hath bestowed upon us, that we should be called the sons of God: therefore the world knoweth us not, because it knew him not. Beloved, now are we the sons of God, and it doth not yet appear what we shall be: but we know that, when he shall appear, we shall be like him; for we shall see him as he is' (1 John 3:1–2). Glorious day! Wonderful day!

Is that how you feel? Do you feel with Paul, 'For now we see through a glass darkly; but then face to face' (1 Corinthians 13:12)? Yes, let us allow Thomas Olivers to speak for us in his great hymn:

> He by Himself hath sworn,
> I on His oath depend;
> I shall, on eagles' wings upborne,
>   To heaven ascend;
>   I shall behold His face,
>   I shall His power adore,
>   And sing the wonders of His grace
> For evermore.
>   *Thomas Olivers*

That is your position, is it not? He has been looking at you, and you have seen him, and I am sure you feel as Henry Collins felt:

> Jesu, what didst Thou find in me
> That Thou hast dealt so lovingly?
> How great the joy that Thou hast brought,
> So far exceeding hope or thought:
> Jesu, my Lord, I Thee adore;
> O make me love Thee more and more.
> *Henry Collins*

God grant that far from being terrified at the thought of the final inspection, we may look forward to it knowing that 'we shall be like him; for we shall see him as he is' (1 John 3:2).

Books by Jack Deere

● *Surprised by the Power of the Spirit*   Much more than an explanation of why one theologian came to believe in signs and wonders for today, this is a profound biblical apologetic, arguing carefully and courteously for the view that the Holy Spirit's supernatural gifts did not cease in New Testament times. And Dr Deere serves Christians on both sides of the debate, as he marks out the pitfalls which threaten to hinder the present-day supernatural ministry of the Holy Spirit.

● *Surprised by the Voice of God*   This book is written for ordinary Christians who want to hear God's voice above the clamour of everyday life. But how do we tell when it is God speaking to us?

Jack Deere brings together inspiring stories from people who have learned to trust God's voice today, his own experiences in teaching and pastoral ministry, and mature biblical teaching.

K
Kingsway Publications

A Godward Life

by John Piper

Every moment we live before the face of God. And before his face, there are no forgotten deeds, no disregarded words, no inconsequential choices. Each moment is an opportunity to live utterly to his glory.

With wisdom and passion John Piper encourages us to savour and to show the supremacy of God in every part of our lives. These brief yet powerful meditations help us to place God at the centre of every thought, every action, every choice, every love – at the centre of all that we are and all that we do.

JOHN PIPER is Senior Pastor of Bethlehem Baptist Church in Minneapolis, Minnesota. He and his wife, Noel, have five children. He is the author of several books, including *A Hunger for God*, *The Pleasures of God* and *The Supremacy of God in Preaching*.

Kingsway Publications

God's Passion for You

by Sam Storms

God delights in you. Does it sound too good to be true? You know you're not good enough. You know you can't earn his love. Yet he loves you with unwavering passion.

Using examples from Scripture, church history and today, Sam Storms reveals the depths of God's pleasure in his people – a pleasure that springs from his very own nature and purposes. God does not wait for us to change before he will love us; yet his love is the very best agent for change in us, once we have let it take root.

Let God's passion for you ignite your passion for him, and for those who do not yet know the riches of God's love.

With a foreword by Mike Bickle.

SAM STORMS is the associate pastor at Metro Christian Fellowship, Kansas City, and a graduate of Dallas Theological Seminary.

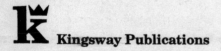

Kingsway Publications